Fanny Crosby
Writer of 8,000 Songs

by

Sandy Dengler

MOODY PRESS

CHICAGO

© 1985 by
THE MOODY BIBLE INSTITUTE
OF CHICAGO

Library of Congress Cataloging in Publication Data

Dengler, Sandy.
  Fanny Crosby, writer of 8,000 songs.

  Summary: A biography of the nineteenth-century
blind woman who wrote more than 8,000 hymns.
  1. Crosby, Fanny, 1820-1915—Juvenile literature.
2. Hymn writers—United States—Biography—Juvenile
literature. [1. Crosby, Fanny, 1820-1915. 2. Hymn
writers. 3. Blind. 4. Physically handicapped]
I. Title. II. Title: Fanny Crosby, writer of eight thousand songs.
BV330.C76D46   1985   264′.2′0924 [B] [92]   84-22695
ISBN 0-8024-2529-1 (pbk.)

9 10 8

Printed in the United States of America

Contents

CHAPTER   PAGE

1. Of Horses and Five-Year-Olds ... 7
2. Of Sea Gulls and Schooners ... 13
3. Of Robins and New York Doctors ... 21
4. Of Dead Trees and Tutors ... 29
5. Of White Roses and Ananias ... 37
6. Of Coach Horses and Open Windows ... 45
7. Of Meadowlarks and Anna ... 53
8. Of Melons and the Dark of Night ... 61
9. Of Skull Bumps and Poetry ... 71
10. Of Fanny Crosby and the Light ... 83
11. Of Elm Trees and Alexander ... 89
12. Of Sunlit Meadows and Mr. Bradbury ... 101
13. Of Mr. Doane and Money for Chicken ... 113
14. Of Butterflies and Prison Walls ... 119
15. Of Violets and Autumn ... 125
16. Of Horses and Very Old Ladies ... 135
    Epilogue ... 141

1

Of Horses and Five-Year-Olds

Spring 1825

Fanny had to hustle to keep up with Peter. His footsteps rustled through the meadow grass ahead of her. The ground beneath her bare feet turned from warm to cold, from firm to squishy. Mud squeezed up between her toes. They were in the low, boggy end of the horse pasture now.

"Peter, are you sure you know where we're going?"

"Here's the fence." Peter slapped his hand against the rough wooden rails. "And there they are. See? I told you we'd find the horses down at this end." The rails rattled, dry and weathered, as he clambered up them.

Fanny scrambled up the rail fence and jumped off on the other side. She was barely five years old, but she could climb any fence Peter could.

She followed close behind him. "Mother and I and maybe my cousin are going clear to New York, Peter. Did you know that?"

"Do now. Gonna stay?"

"No. Just visit some friends of mother's named

Smith. And talk to some doctors. Then we'll come home again."

Peter grunted.

He did not seem much interested, so Fanny said no more about it. The coming journey frightened her anyway; she didn't like to think about it.

A horse snorted just ahead of her. It nickered.

Fanny spoke softly. "Hello, Beauty. How are you, you lovely creature? Here's a carrot. Come to Fanny." She stood still and broke off a piece of carrot. She extended her hand out flat, palm up. The carrot chunk rested there only a moment. The horse snorted again, right near her hand. Its warm breath washed past her fingers. Thick, velvety lips tickled her palm as Beauty accepted his bribe. Fanny held out another carrot chunk. It was swept away. Huge teeth crunched, *grutch grutch grutch.*

"I have them both. Here's Beauty's rope. It goes around his throat and loops over his nose." Peter slapped the rope end into Fanny's hand. He gave her a boost, and she squirmed up onto Beauty's back.

The rough rope jerked in her hand as Beauty shook his head. They started off across the meadow at a walk. With hard bones beneath and soft, sun-warmed skin on top, the unique feel of Beauty's back intrigued Fanny. She loved his slippery hide. She loved his constant rambling motion. She loved the moist breeze on her face, and the spring sun's radiance. She ran her fingers down Beauty's soft, bulgy forequarters, across his rock-hard withers.

Peter rode up beside her. "Hold your rope tighter, Fan, or the loop will slip off his nose, and you won't be able—oh, no! It did!"

The rope in her hand went slack. Beauty's muscles bunched beneath Fanny's knees. He broke into a trot. Fanny had no way to stop him. He lunged forward into a rocking-horse canter. His long, sleek neck stretched out.

Fanny dropped the rope and grabbed the coarse mane in both hands. She drew her knees up and clamped them tight. She tucked down close to his neck and buried her face in his mane. No doubt he would run full tilt into the shed, and the doorway was very low. She must keep her head down. The smooth, slender neck pulsed against her cheek. The huge feet pounded soft on the grass, now loud on bare ground. They were in the barnyard.

His stride shortened, got jerky. Warm sun changed instantly into cold shadow. Fanny clamped harder with her legs and heels as Beauty bobbed to an uneasy halt. He seemed to love running as much as she loved riding him at a run. She slid off his back. Her feet hit loose, dry straw. They were in the big feed stall.

"Frances Jane Crosby! You bad little girl!" Mrs. Shaw's raspy voice sounded as though Fanny had just committed the world's most horrible sin. "Shame on you for such behavior! Shame on you for disgracing your poor widowed mother so! Shame! Shame!"

"Yes'm. I'm sorry, mum." Fanny mumbled. After all, Beauty did belong to Mrs. Shaw. Still, Mrs. Shaw apparently never rode him; at least, that's what Peter said. Fanny bumped against the manger. She grabbed the top of the stall divider and used the manger for a step up. As she squirmed and tumbled over the divider into the barn walkway, Mrs. Shaw's pudgy hand grabbed hers.

Mrs. Shaw pulled her down the walkway in jerks. "This isn't the first time you've been caught riding on horses, but it had better be the last. Do you understand? The very idea!"

They popped from coolness into warmth. Sun swarmed across Fanny's face. Mrs. Shaw stopped, but she still gripped Fanny's wrist. "Now where is that rascal Peter? He must take you home right now."

Fanny struggled to pull free. "I don't need Peter. I can get home just fine. I'll do it myself!" Belatedly, she remembered her manners and added, "Thank you, ma'am."

"Peter? Peter!" The shrill voice bellowed. Then Mrs. Shaw sighed. "Honestly, you two! Well, I don't have time to take you home. I'll just have to take you out to the road and send you on your way." Off she went, marching along lickety-split. Fanny stumbled; she had to trot to keep up. How could such a heavy lady walk so fast?

The gravel in Mrs. Shaw's lane was looser than the dirt in the road, and coarser. They stepped out onto the road. To get home from here Fanny must keep the sun on her right cheek.

"Here's the road." Mrs. Shaw gripped both Fanny's shoulders and turned her around. The sun toasted her right cheek. Mrs. Shaw gave Fanny a little push to send her on her way. "There you go, young lady. Now don't let me catch you around the horses again, do you hear?"

"Yes'm," Fanny muttered. She started walking quickly, keeping the hard-packed dirt beneath her feet, staying clear of the loose roadside dirt and weeds.

Mrs. Shaw's voice behind her got farther and farther away, but it didn't slow up a bit. "Remember! Never again! Shame on you, Fanny Crosby! Whoever heard of such a thing? Your mother should have taught you that little blind girls cannot ride horses!"

2

Of Sea Gulls and Schooners

April 1825

April, like January, has two faces. One face is warm, bright sun and springtime smells. But let the sun drift behind one small cloud, and the other face turns—the sour face. The air instantly hangs heavy with damp coldness left over from winter. Fanny huddled in the corner of a jouncing farm wagon and wished the sun would come back out again. She did not like April days that turned dreary. She did not like riding in the back of a farm wagon with no springs. With every rut and hole in the road, the wagon bed would drop out from under her, then come slamming up against her. And it was hard. Even the sacks of potatoes Fanny leaned against were hard.

She thought about this long journey to New York and felt worse and worse. Mother said a surgeon might be able to help Fanny see. The surgeon would cut around her eyes somehow. Fanny had cut herself before. She knew how much it hurt. And to let a doctor stand there and cut and cut and poke and—Fanny shuddered.

Her mother sat up on the wagon seat beside

the driver. The wagon seat had springs under it to cushion the jolts. Why couldn't they put the whole wagon on springs?

Mother spoke suddenly. "Why, Mr. Slade. You have a newspaper on the floor here. May I read it?"

"Aye. Been there awhile, but welcome."

The newspaper rattled. "It's dated February. That's only two months old. Oh, wait; eighteen twenty-four. It's a *year* and two months old. Ah, well, better than nothing, I suppose." Mother fell silent again. The newspaper rattled every time the wagon bounced.

Fanny shifted. The sacks of potatoes were much too hard and lumpy to be comfortable. She stood up and hooked her arms over the back of the seat. Her chin rested near mother's shoulder. "How long before we get there?"

"Half hour," Mr. Slade replied. "Can't ye see the river stretching away out there?" His voice dropped. "Sorry, Miss Fanny. Forgot ye can't see nothing."

"I can see light and dark a little."

The newspaper crunched into Mother's lap. "Fanny, it's just beautiful. Give me your hand. In the far distance are some rounded hills shaped like this." She bent Fanny's fingers into a gentle curl. "Along one shore they stop abruptly, very steep. They're called bluffs. And the river rolls at the base of them. I've never seen such a wide river! It's almost like a long, long lake."

"Can you see ships on the river?"

"All manner of boats. Sailing boats, rowboats, fishing boats, rafts. The Hudson is an important river, you know."

Fanny's breastbone tickled. "And we shall ride on a big boat."

"And we shall ride in a boat." Mother's voice trailed away. She was worrying again.

"Connecticut is a real long way from New York. If we lived in New York we wouldn't have to travel for days. Why do we live in Connecticut?"

"Because your grandparents Sylvanus and Eunice and your great-grandparents Isaac and Mercy were there, and your father, John, is buried there. It's your home, and mine." Her voice was getting a bit impatient. Fanny had best not ask more questions for a while.

The wagon jerked and clattered more than usual. Suddenly Fanny heard a poem! A gaggle of children's voices was reciting a poem somewhere off to the left.

"Mother! Listen!"

"We're passing a schoolhouse, Fanny. We're coming into town."

"I love poems! Do you suppose they're reading or are they reciting?"

"I wouldn't know, dear."

"If the doctors can fix my eyes, then I can read, huh, Mother?"

The wagon's iron tires clanked on stone, and the ride smoothed out. They were crossing paving stones of some sort. Dogs barked and people shouted. Someone hawked hot pastries beside the street. The wagon stopped. Fanny smelled a dank, penetrating odor she had never smelled before. They must be right down by the docks. She forgot about fearing what doctors might do. They would ride in an elegant, graceful ship all the way to New York! They would sail from this evening through tomorrow evening, a long, long ride.

"Ho, Captain Green!" Mr. Slade shouted so suddenly Fanny jumped. "Cap'n, this yere's y'r fare, Mercy Crosby. And here's 'er daughter, Fanny."

"In your service, madame." The captain's voice was gruff and deep and rumbly. But Fanny could hear the lilt in it. This was no grumpy old man. This was what Mother called a pussycat, like Old David who lived down the road from them. David liked to sound cross and mean, but he always melted when Fanny spoke to him.

Fanny climbed down off the back of the wagon. Her feet met massive boards like those in a barn floor. One of Mr. Slade's horses stamped its foot. The *clomp* rang hollow. Mother had told her the ship would be tied up at a wharf. This must be the wharf. The captain, the farmer, and Mother were all discussing weather and potatoes. Fanny paid no attention. She was trying to sort out a thousand sounds and smells she had never heard or smelled before.

A calloused hand grasped hers. "So you're little Fanny. I'm the mate, Mr. Tanner. Call me Joe. Welcome aboard, lass." The hand led her forward. She walked now on thinner boards. Water slopped somewhere below her; the board beneath her bobbed from their weight. And now she was stepping onto a floor that was firm and yet not firm. Curious.

Joe placed her hand on a smooth banisterlike rail. "We'll be putting out shortly, missy. Just stand here and y'll be able to hear everything going on without getting in the way."

"What's that mewing sound, please?"

"Sea gulls, missy."

"What do they look like?"

He took her wrists and spread her arms. "About this long beak to tail, and about this long wingtip to wingtip. All wings and appetite. Y'll find 'em anywhere there's fish or garbage. They'll soar in the air, or perch on a pier post, or float like a duck in the water. I must go now. The clunking y'll hear is the gangplank coming aboard. Then y'll listen for the captain's calls and mine as we cast off and hoist sail." He put her hand back on the rail and hurried off.

A sea gull mewed as it swept by. Parts all over the ship began to creak. Some noises sounded like the block and tackle used to hoist carcasses at butchering time. The rail vibrated beneath her hand. She heard the gangplank come clunking aboard.

"Cast off the stern," the captain shouted nearby.

From behind Fanny someone shouted a reply. Joe called out, and the voice answered him also. Yet, Fanny didn't understand a word. How could they make the ship work when they spoke to each other unintelligibly?

The deck lurched, and she grabbed the rail with both hands. The ship wallowed. The whole ship—rail, deck, and creaks—leaned gently and firmly to the left. A snapping sound like canvas rugs being shaken out—that must be the sails. Then the ship leaned forward, steady and powerful, like a lumbering old plow horse.

The breeze picked up. Fanny turned around so that it blew in her face instead of pushing on the back of her hair. The ship leaned farther left, as if it would tip. Men shouted, canvas snapped, blocks creaked, the wind changed abruptly. The ship leveled off—well, almost. It kept a slight tilt. So this was sailing. Oh, Fanny loved it!

They weren't even leaving the gulls behind. She heard a whole group of them mewing and squabbling at the back of the ship. They must be able to fly fast to keep up.

"Here ye go, missy. I'll show ye to y'r quarters." Joe's rough hand clasped hers.

She followed him across the leaning deck. "How many miles have we gone so far?"

Joe roared. "Miles? A couple hundred yards at most. We barely be into the channel and headed south. 'Twill be a bit rough, the way the breeze lies. Ye aren't subject to seasickness, I trust."

"I don't know. I've never been on a boat before."

"Neither has y'r dear mother, I daresay. She's lying down till her stomach settles." Joe stopped. "Come to think about it, let's stay on deck here and let 'er rest." He changed directions, and they walked uphill. Suddenly Joe scooped her up and set her down on a hard, scratchy coil of rope.

"Now, missy," Joe crooned, "hear me! Y're never to come out here on deck 'less one of us is with you. Should ye tip overboard we'd never find ye. 'Tis a rule. A strict law. Understand?"

"Yes, sir." Fanny sat awhile listening to the chorus of creaks. None was familiar. The touch of Joe's calloused hand on hers was foreign. The sea gulls weren't mewing; they were whining mournfully. This ship was very much like a horse—something big and powerful that Fanny could not control. It was carrying her away from home, away from Grandmother Eunice. The strange sounds and smells made her feel lost.

She wanted to be home. Her eyes burned. She sniffled. Joe's alien hand squeezed hers tighter.

"Wait!" Fanny sat up straight. "That smell!" This was no shipboard odor. Fanny turned this way and that. "There's a cow here!"

"Aye. A farmer's taking his cow down to Staten Island. But how did ye know?"

Fanny hopped down off the scratchy coil. She hurried toward the smell, keeping the breeze in her face. She bumped into only a few things, and they were small enough to get around. Here were boards nailed together to form a crude stanchion. She heard a gentle *munch*. She slipped between the boards, reaching. Her fingers brushed smooth, warm hide stretched over huge cow ribs. The skin rippled beneath her touch.

"A cow." Fanny ran both hands along the twitchy hide. Here was the flat neck, the shoulder, the flanks. She felt the bulging milk vein across the cow's underbelly. "And she's a good milker, too."

Joe laughed behind her. "Y're right, missy. Indeed, she needs milking just now, but her owner's indisposed. I don't suppose you're a milkmaid."

"No. My hands aren't strong enough." It felt so good to wrap her arms around something familiar in this alien world. Fanny snuggled her cheek in against the placid neck. "But I shall keep the cow company until you find someone to milk her. I'll stay with her the whole trip, so she doesn't feel lonely. I'll bet she's very lonely, don't you think?"

Joe's voice rumbled gently, thoughtfully. "I think at least one of you is."

3

Of Robins and New York Doctors

Spring 1825

Fanny sat very still. She laced her fingers together in her lap to keep her hands from shaking. She was sitting on a heavy oak table, her legs dangling over the side. Not one doctor but two hovered close around her, like bees around a flower.

The one named Dr. Mott said, "Without raising your head, look at the ceiling, please. That's right. Now without moving, look down at the floor." He snapped his fingers. "Look toward that sound." Fingers snapped on the other side of her head. "Now there. Good girl!"

Would they grab her and start cutting? They were both so close, and she couldn't see to duck away.

The other, Dr. Delafield, spoke. "What do you see, Frances?"

"Light."

"And now?"

"Nothing. No light. Dark."

"How about peripheral? Dextrad of the right eye there?" When Dr. Mott used words like that, Fanny knew he wasn't talking to her.

Dr. Delafield asked, "Now what do you see?"

"A little light."

"That's all?" Dr. Delafield sniffed. "So much for peripheral."

Dr. Mott's huge hands hooked under her arms and lifted her high. He set her feet on the floor. "You've been very cooperative, Frances. I wish all our patients were as easy to work with as you are."

"Thank you, sir." Fanny smiled outside, but inside she was terrified. He called her a patient. Would they grab her now?

"You may go out in the waiting room, Frances. We have quite a selction of toys there."

Toys in a doctor's office? A warm hand took Fanny's and led her forward.

Dr. Mott stopped. "Sit here, if you like." The hand left.

Fanny folded her knees and settled onto the waxed hardwood floor. Cautiously she reached out. Dr. Mott was right; they had a wonderful selection of toys! She groped eagerly in all directions.

She was surrounded by all manner of things. She had so few toys at home. It was almost worth the trip to New York just to play with all these marvelous things. Her left hand found a little sailboat.

Sailing. Fanny grinned. It had been a glorious trip coming down the river, and they would sail again upriver to get home. She thought of the funny stories the captain told. She thought about the poems she recited for him and the songs she sang. He seemed to like them very much. And the warm, gentle cow—they did find someone to milk her. And that evening Mother felt well enough to make a custard with the fresh milk. Delicious!

She clutched the boat close and let her right hand explore. Was this a lamb? It was a wooden toy of some sort covered with fleece—yes, a lamb on wheels. Fanny had owned a live lamb a year or two ago. "Mary had a little lamb...." She recited the poem inside her head. Had Mary ever been knocked over by her big, rough, ill-tempered lamb? Fanny had. Mother never explained why the lamb simply disappeared one day. But a week later they ate lamb chops. Fanny's lamb was gone, and yet the poem was alive inside her head. The poem was older than a hundred lambs, yet it lived—in a way. It was just as well—she liked poems much better than lambs.

Dr. Mott called from a doorway, "Frances, come in, please."

Fearfully, Fanny stood up and walked to the voice. The firm hand led her forward. Was this when—?

Dr. Delafield spoke. "Mrs. Crosby, her eyes are twice damaged. The clear portion in the very front, the cornea, is scarred from the mustard poultice applied by that doctor. But the nerves, the portion deep inside, are also damaged, apparently from the infection itself. Even if there were some miraculous way to clear the corneas, her vision would not return. Not fully."

Mother's voice was flat, despairing. "Then surgery would do nothing for her."

"Nothing. The muscles are atrophying but otherwise are in good condition. The problems are inside, where we can't reach."

"There is no hope."

"Now just a moment, Mrs. Crosby. There's no hope for her sight, but you certainly mustn't give up on the girl. She's clever and quick. I assure you, with encouragement she'll get on fine."

"Forever blind." It was as if Mother didn't even hear him.

Fanny crossed to her. She found her mother's shoulder and laid her hand on it. When Mother sounded so sad and depressed it made Fanny sad and depressed. But Fanny had no idea how to cheer her up. She didn't know what to say.

Mother stood up abruptly and grabbed Fanny's hand. "Thank you, doctors. I appreciate very much your service and advice. Good day."

"Good day, Mrs. Crosby. God bless you. And God bless you, little Frances Jane."

"Thank you, sirs." Fanny walked toward the door. Suddenly she stopped; her hand slipped out of Mother's. She turned. "And thank you very much for letting me play with your toys. They're lovely toys."

"You are most welcome."

Mother snatched her hand and pulled her along. They walked a long hall. Some sort of doorkeeper must be holding the door for them; the fresh spring breeze swept over Fanny's face before the sun touched her. They walked down five stone steps. And now they started the long walk that would take them back to the Smiths'.

New York was full of more people than Fanny had ever dreamed of. Footsteps swarmed constantly on all sides. A hundred voices passed, all talking about a thousand different things. Horses clipped up and down the streets by the dozen. Wagons creaked; light carriages and gigs whispered through the dust.

A scratchy wool shawl brushed her cheek and bumped her shoulder. A woman snapped impatiently, "Watch where you're going, little girl!"

Fanny's mother clamped her hand tighter. Her fingers were icy.

A boy called, "Extra! Extra! Read all about it!"

How Fanny wished she could! But blind people could never read. "Mother? What's an extra? Read about what?"

"The newspaper puts out an extra edition if something important happens."

"Don't you want to read it? It might be interesting."

"Nothing in this city could possibly interest us. Nothing." Mother charged on forward. Fanny heard her sniffle. She was crying again. Fanny felt somehow to blame.

Somewhere to the left a robin started singing. Fanny might be a four-day journey from her warm, soft bed, but the robins in New York sang exactly like the robins outside her bedroom window. They stopped suddenly for traffic; freight wagons rumbled by in front of them.

The robin shifted to a new and closer singing post. Fanny moved her free hand out to the length of a robin, then to a sea gull. Gulls were twice as big, yet they sounded no stronger. Had Grandma Eunice ever seen a sea gull? Fanny would have to ask.

They marched out across the street, scuffling

through dirt turned to powder by a million wheels and hooves.

"Do you like New York?" Fanny asked.

"No!"

"I do."

"Noisy. Dirty. Full of stuck-up city people. You're a country girl, Fan, same as me. Put foolish notions out of your head."

"What foolish notions?"

"Being something you're not. Thinking you can get citified. Or that you're as good as anyone else. You aren't. I'm not. And you'll save yourself a lot of grief if you accept that right now, while you're young."

Fanny said no more. Mother was upset and talking was therefore useless. Fanny felt terribly mixed up herself. She was extremely glad there would be no doctors cutting into her. And yet, she was extremely sad that nothing, cutting or otherwise, would help her blindness. There would be no surgery, but neither would there be any reading. She would never know what a robin really looked like.

A sparrow chipped in bushes beside her. Fanny reached toward the sound. The bush was just starting to leaf out with tender green fuzz-tips. April. Spring. April was just as much April here in New York as it was in Connecticut.

Fanny's mother might not like crowds of people, but Fanny loved bustle. She loved people. She couldn't stand just sitting idle. Surely there were all manner of things to do in a city this big. New York had robins, spring leaves, sparrows—everything the country had, and more. Fanny would like to come here to live as soon as she was grown up and making her own way.

Her good cheer froze to sadness. Make her own way? A blind girl? To make one's way through life, especially through a city life, one should be able to read and write and cipher. One surely must be able to see.

And Fanny Crosby never would.

4

Of Dead Trees and Tutors

Summer 1829

Fanny leaned against the rough, solid tree trunk and listened to the leaves rustling overhead. The village green here in Ridgefield was bigger than the one in North Salem—more open, more distant, not nearly so friendly. Everything about Ridgefield was different and unfriendly. Fanny felt so alone. Why did Mother have to move here, anyway?

Before, Fanny could visit Grandma Eunice every day. She was too far away to see at all now. Fanny and Mother used to live in a little cottage of their own. They lived in a fine big house now, but it wasn't theirs. It belonged to the Hawleys, and Mother was the Hawleys' new maid. Now Fanny must come and go softly, carefully, lest she disturb the master and mistress of the house.

Her mother was a housekeeper. What was Fanny? Nothing. She couldn't be a maid or seamstress or housekeeper—she had no eyes. She couldn't be a school pupil—no eyes. She had tried going to school; it just didn't work. So here she was, nine years old, a nothing. The wind picked up and complained among the noisy leaves.

School was ended for the day; children's voices came laughing across the green.

"Hey Fran-sess! Let's play blind man's bluff! Guess who's the blind man!" His name was Sid something. He never teased just to tease. He teased to hurt, deliberately. She ignored him.

Clumpy feet galumphed past her. An unseen hand grabbed her hair and yanked it so hard her head snapped. Fanny felt like pasting old Sid a good one, but she didn't try. For one thing, you're supposed to turn the other cheek. For another, she almost always missed, and then the children around her would laugh all the harder.

The feet clumped by again, and Fanny's sash came untied instantly. Sid was fast becoming difficult to turn the other cheek to.

Here came the feet again.

"Stop it!" Fanny lashed out, but Sid had ducked away. A half dozen children were laughing all around her.

The clodhopper feet were coming again. Suddenly Sid grunted, the sound you make when you run into something so hard you knock your breath out. He splacked to the ground.

A cheerful boy's voice purred, "Why, Sid! I'm so sorry! Here; let me help you to your feet. I really must watch where I'm going. I'm so clumsy; not agile, like you. Here, can I dust you off? Let me help—why, Sid, where are you going?"

Half a dozen soprano voices howled with laughter, and for once they weren't laughing at Fanny. Sid's heavy feet stomped away toward the street. A small voice cried, "Tag, Jeremiah! You're it!" And just that fast a game was started.

A small hand hit Fanny's shoulder. "You're it!"

Fanny grinned. They didn't know that she excelled at tag back in North Salem. She walked forward until she was well clear of the oak trees. The scythed grass was thicker here; she could hear better. She paused a moment, listening. She took three quick steps to her left. As she zigzagged forward she heard the faintest whisper of grass to her right, almost behind her. She lunged at the sound, her hand out.

She connected. "Tag! You're it!"

"Hey! How did you—?" The voice laughed. It was a boy maybe two inches taller than Fanny. He ran off. Someone ran toward her, and she jumped aside. Her ears told her there were seven players, but three of them were little—no more than six or seven years old. No, here came an eighth. She could tell by the determined way the person darted that he/she was It. She leaped aside and dashed forward.

Eight voices screamed "Stop!" at once. Too late—Ridgefield Green had one too many trees.

One moment, Fanny was running. The next moment she sprawled in the grass unable to breathe. She couldn't think clearly, either. She had run into trees before but never this hard. Why would the city fathers ever plant a tree out here in the middle? Greens were supposed to be open. She'd better try to stand up.

Strong hands gripped her arms and helped her up. "Did you hurt yourself?" It was the boy who had tangled with Sid.

"No—I don't—I doubt—" Fanny's wits came trickling back a bit at a time. She took a few deep breaths and laid her hand on the boy's arm. "Tag. You are it, kind sir."

"I've been foxed!" The hands left her arms instantly. The grass rustled. "Tag! You're it, Minerva." The voice turned back toward Fanny. "And I have to get home and haul the wood in before supper."

"Yes, it's late. I'd better go home, too." Fanny took another deep breath. Her ribs ached.

"I'll walk with you partway. My name's Sylvester Main. Most call me Vet. Your name is Frances, and your mother works for Hawleys, right?"

"Most people call me Fanny." She listened a moment for the sounds of traffic and started toward the street. "I don't know how that happened. I never run into trees; the shade warns me."

Vet laughed. "It's the tree's fault. You see, there isn't any shade. That old tree's been dead for years."

"Then why is it—?" Fanny stopped talking. The matter was done. She knew where it was now; she wouldn't run into it again. Vet told a joke, and they walked on laughing and chatting. On the outside Fanny was merry. On the inside she burned with shame. If she weren't blind, Sid wouldn't tease her. Children wouldn't laugh. She wouldn't run into trees, living or dead.

Vet left her at the Hawleys' gate and continued on whistling. Fanny hopped up the porch steps and dragged the heavy door open. She must be careful not to disturb Mrs. Hawley; Mother must have said that a million times.

"There you are!" Mrs. Hawley's voice made Fanny jump. The lady of the house was in the drawing room, the first door right down the hallway. "Come in here, please, Frances."

Fanny paused in the doorway. She had never been in this room before. She didn't know where the furniture was. She moved forward, her hands out, onto a carpet.

"Take this chair, please. I wish to talk to you."

Ah! Now Fanny knew just where the lady was. She calculated about where the chair should be. She walked straight, hands in front, until she touched polished wood. She ran her fingers across it—a chair back. "This chair, mum?"

"Very good, Frances. It's extraordinary, how well you get about. You're nine years old now."

"Yes'm."

"Has anyone ever told you what lovely dark hair you have? That curl is natural, isn't it?"

"Yes'm. Mother says our station in life and the way we look are both God's doing, and we shouldn't change either one."

"Remarkable woman, your mother. I understand your grandmother is also a fine Christian lady. That she reads Scripture to you."

"Yes'm. She helps me memorize it."

"Oh?" Mrs. Hawley sounded surprised. "Whole passages?"

"Whole books, yes'm."

"Do you have a favorite portion in Scripture?"

"The Psalms, mum. Grandma says they're the finest poetry ever written, and I do love poetry."

"You enjoy hearing poetry read."

"I write some, too, mum."

"Indeed." Was Mrs. Hawley pleased or displeased? Fanny couldn't tell. "I trust your mother reads to you often."

"No, mum. She's, ah—very busy, you know."

Fanny didn't want to say that Mother never bothered, that Mother had no hope. Mother herself never said that, but that was how things were.

"I see." Mrs. Hawley sat quiet for several minutes. Should Fanny speak? Leave? She sat still with her hands in her lap, quiet on the outside and jumpy inside.

"Frances, you're a remarkable young lady. I believe God has special plans for you. I believe He has permitted your blindness in order to serve His purposes, whatever they are."

"Our pastor says that, too, Mum."

"Yes. Therefore I see a Christian duty to help prepare you for whatever God's plan may be. I shall be your tutor. Do you know what a tutor is?"

"Um, ah—a schoolmaster without a school?"

Mrs. Hawley chuckled. "A teacher. You say you enjoy poetry. We shall take that as our signal of God's intent and start there. What your dear grandmother began I shall continue, with your mother's assent."

Fanny decided vaguely that she was being honored by the lady's attention, but it sounded a bit scary.

"Have you attended school?"

"A little, now and then." (Should Fanny say this, or not? Oh, why not?) "The schoolmaster said I am uneducable."

"Do you understand what he meant?"

"Yes'm. He thinks I'm too stupid to learn."

Mrs. Hawley snorted. "You can't be too stupid when you pronounce 'uneducable' correctly and define it. Come to me this afternoon, Frances, and we shall commence. You are dismissed."

Fanny stood up. "Thank you, mum." She curtsied as her mother had taught her and aimed herself toward the door. She walked straight out into the hallway, her fingers brushing the door jamb. She turned right, toward the stairs. What did Mrs. Hawley mean by "taking up Grandma's work"? She could never replace Grandma.

Fanny climbed the stairs to the little attic room. Mother had left the window open; a cool afternoon breeze made the chintz curtains nudge each other and whisper. Fanny dragged a chair to the window. She sat down and leaned both elbows on the sill.

Ridgefield Green was not like North Salem's. Ridgefield's sounds and smells were not like North Salem's. In fact, Ridgefield smelled a little like New York. Fanny smiled. New York. Now there was the place to go! It was a huge town. It should be full of poems and poets. She slipped off the chair to her knees and clasped her hands in approved prayer style.

"Dear Father in heaven. I know You're getting tired of hearing this, but I'm praying it again. Please send me to school so I can learn to read somehow. Nothing is supposed to be impossible for You. The pastor says so. So will You please let me learn, like other children? P.S. New York would be a very nice place to do it. Bless Grandma Eunice and Mother and the Hawleys. Amen." She started to her feet and dropped down again. "Oh, yes. And Vet. He's a very nice boy to come to my aid like that. Amen."

She plunked back into her chair and draped herself across the sill again. Her feet wanted somewhere to go—or tidings to bring, as Scripture says. Her hands diddled nervously, wanting something to do ("The Devil finds work for idle hands," said Mother). Her mind jumped and fluttered like a wild bird in a cage. Her soul beat its wings against the bars, trapped.

She could see no purpose, divine or otherwise, in being blind. She could see no job a blind girl could fill. That depressed her. She wanted so many things she knew she would never have, and that depressed her still more. God was taxing her spirit sorely.

Or was He? Perhaps He was simply ignoring her. Lately she had become aware of an empty spot deep inside. It was a vacant place, an unfilled place, a lack. Perhaps the empty spot inside Fanny was filled in other people by their vision. Perhaps it was an empty place for the blind only. Or perhaps learning filled it. If the emptiness were either vision or learning, Fanny was doomed. And that was a most depressing thought.

In a tree outside the window a robin warbled in zigzag—up and down, up and down. The Bible promised that God watches over sparrows and therefore probably robins also. Surely He watched over little Fanny Crosby. Did robins feel the emptiness? Surely not. No one who sang that sweetly could ever feel empty.

Besides, robins don't have to know how to read.

5

Of White Roses and Ananias

Summer 1829

"Nothing warms the old bones like sun on a hot summer day." That's what Mother always said, and Fanny agreed. The summer sun splashed brilliance all over the Hawleys' rose garden. The subtle aroma of flowers percolated in under the trees. Fanny stretched out with her face in the shade. Sunshine makes freckles; besides, it bothered Fanny's eyes sometimes. All the rest of her basked in warm sun. It soaked through her dark stockings and black skirt.

"Ah, sun," Fanny purred. "Glorious."

"I suppose so." Beside Fanny, her friend Daisy's skirt rustled. "But sun darkens the skin so, and sun-darkened skin just isn't fashionable anymore, you know. Ten years ago, maybe, but not now. And sun fades the draperies terribly. I rather wish there were no sun at all."

"Oh, Daisy! Think what happens to a plant left in the dark too long. All the plants in the world would die if there were no sun at all. No trees—"

"No wooden desks," Daisy interrupted. "No rul-

ers for the school master to rap your knuckles
with. I wouldn't mind."

"—no grass—"

"No chiggers. No green stains on your best
white dress. No little green snakes for your
brother to find and bring in the house."

"—no vegetables—"

"Goody."

"—no flowers."

"Mm. Now that would be difficult. Very well, I
concede. The sun may stay."

Fanny hooted. "How generous of you, Queen
Daisy! Any other decrees, while you're in such a
benevolent mood?"

"I should think that since I gave the sun permission to stay, I should reap some of the sun's
rewards. Too bad we can't pick any of the roses
here."

"Oh, but we can. Mrs. Hawley says I may
have whatever roses I wish except for the white
ones over there." She waved an arm in the gen-
eral direction.

"Then let's!" Daisy hopped to her feet.

Fanny stood up and stepped out into the sun.
She followed Daisy until Daisy walked right on
through the arbor. Fanny paused there. Warm
dots of sun danced about on her face as the
leaves above her moved in the breeze. The arch-
ing arbor trapped all the rose smells into one
delicious floating pool of sweet aroma. She followed Daisy's babbling voice out into the garden.

Fanny stopped near Daisy and cupped her
hand around a bloom. The delicate petals brushed
her fingers, feather soft. The lovely fragrance
surrounded the blossom like a cloud. When an
aroma was this strong, couldn't you see it just a

little? Fanny had asked Grandma Eunice that. Grandma said no. You can't see smells any more than you can hear them. And yet it was so striking, so beautiful—perhaps eyes sharper than Grandma's could see it.

Daisy wandered casually along the trellises, her skirts whispering. "This pink rose is lovely, but it's rather small. Ah. Here's a yellow beauty. No; some little bug ate a hole in one petal. Here's another—too far opened. You want the bud at its peak, just unfolding. Here's one—scarlet. Reminds one too much of blood." She ambled on.

"Your choice is all backward. Here you are finding something wrong with every flower. Instead of finding fault, you should have trouble picking one because they're all so perfect."

"Honestly, Fan." Daisy's voice pouted. "You look on the bright side so constantly it gets wearying after a while."

"Be picky if you wish. I'll have a lovely bouquet of roses while you're still trying to find one you like."

"Here, Daisy offered. "I'll pick some for you."

"No. Thank you, but I'll do it myself." Fanny's fingers flew from rose to rose. Here was one just opening, as Daisy had described. But it didn't have much aroma at all yet—it was too young. Fanny passed it by. Here was another, floating in a halo of fragrance. Fanny snapped it off just below the second leaf. And here was another. Fanny, of course, cared nothing for color. She chose the loveliest with her nose. Soon she had a bouquet of six.

Daisy was wandering back this way. "Really, Fan, I cannot choose. Which rose shall I pick as my reward? Wait! I found it! Half open, a perfect bud. Ah, the fragrance. Ah, the texture. Fit for a queen—namely, me."

Fanny sniffed the bloom and brushed her lips across its delicate softness. "Lovely! What color is it?"

"White. Pure white, like driven snow."

"Then you can't have it, remember? Mrs. Hawley said—"

"Mrs. Hawley has a whole bush full of these white roses," Daisy interrupted. "And I happen to know she's not the selfish sort. She'll never miss just one. She won't even see that it's gone."

"But she said we shouldn't, so we shouldn't."

"All right, if you insist. We shouldn't. But you're not going to tell if we do, are you?" Daisy patted Fanny's head. "Really, this is my choice, my only choice. Right here."

Fanny sniffed again. Why do forbidden roses smell so fine? "This one only, and no more?"

"Just that one."

Fanny hesitated only a moment. Carefully she bent the stem over at the second leaf and snapped it off. "Go home through the back gate so Mrs. Hawley doesn't see you with that."

"If it'll make you feel better."

They continued on around the rose garden and Fanny gathered three more for her bouquet. Daisy left, then—through the back gate. Fanny must go in, too. It was nearly time for her day's lesson. The cheerful sun still warmed her back, but Fanny didn't feel cheerful. The thorns on that forbidden rose pricked her conscience. She shouldn't have done it. Yet, Daisy was right (Daisy was older; she ought to be right). The selfless Mrs. Hawley wouldn't mind just one of a whole bushful.

Fanny stopped by the kitchen and dug a vase out of the corner cupboard. She filled it with water from the bucket by the stove and arranged her bouquet with the tallest in the middle. For a fleeting moment she wished she could see the colors of her fragrant mound. She carried the bouquet to her room and set it beside the bed. Soon her whole room would smell like the inside of a rose. She snatched up her Bible and hurried downstairs to the drawing room.

"There you are." Mrs. Hawley sat by the window. Fanny crossed to her and sat down on the cushion in the window bay. Warm sun flooded over her. Her Bible lifted out of her lap; the pages whispered.

"Fanny?" Mrs. Hawley cleared her throat. "Do you know who picked the pretty white rose from the bush yonder?"

"No, mum," Fanny murmured. Her heart thumped. Had Mrs. Hawley seen her? Probably not, or she would not have asked; she would have accused. Fanny waited for the next question, biting her lip.

But Mrs. Hawley asked no more questions. "Our lesson today will be from the book of Acts, chapter four verse thirty-two through five, eleven. To begin:

> And the multitude of them that believed were of one heart and of one soul: neither said any of them that ought of the things which he possessed were his own; but they had all things in common.

"That means, Fanny, that every person shared all he had. One man might own a donkey, for example, but any man could use that donkey freely." She continued reading.

Like roses, Fanny mused. The roses were Mrs. Hawley's, but any person could enjoy them.

> . . . possessors of lands or houses sold them, and brought the prices of the things that were sold, and laid them down at the apostles' feet: and distribution was made unto every man according as he had need.

"That means, Fanny, that the wealthy sold their holdings in order to provide the money to feed all the believers." She continued.

Daisy had said Mrs. Hawley was not selfish. Surely, if believers needed the money, Mrs. Hawley would be just as generous and sell her home to feed them. So would Fanny, when she grew up.

> But a certain man named Ananias, with Sapphira his wife, sold a possession, and kept back part of the price, his wife also being privy to it, and brought a certain part, and laid it at the apostles' feet.

"In other words, Ananias lied to the apostles about his gift. 'Being privy to it' means that the wife was aware of what Ananias was doing."

> But Peter said, Ananias, why hath Satan filled thine heart to lie to the Holy Spirit . . .

Fanny's stomach churned. Mrs. Hawley—and the Bible—attributed Ananias's lie directly to Satan. Jesus Himself called Satan the father of lies. And Fanny had just told a whopper!

Mrs. Hawley read on:

... Thou hast not lied unto men, but unto God. And Ananias hearing these words fell down, and gave up the ghost:

"Or put more plainly, Fanny, he dropped dead on the spot." She read on, but Fanny heard only the word "fear" in the next sentence.

Fear? Fanny could hear her own heart beating. Would she drop dead over a silly white rose? It didn't even smell that good! Now Mrs. Hawley was reading about how Sapphira came back and didn't know what had happened to Ananias.

Then Peter said unto her, How is it that ye have agreed together to tempt the Spirit of the Lord? behold, the feet of them which have buried thy husband are at the door, and shall carry thee out. Then she fell down straightway at his feet, and yielded up the ghost.

"Now, Fanny, Ananias was clearly guilty of lying. But why did Sapphira die as well?"

"Uh—" Fanny had to think hard. She had not been listening well. "Uh, she was privy to it. She was in on it."

"Do you suppose Ananias's fatal sin was keeping back part of the money or was it lying about it?"

"The, uh—lying about it?"

"Apparently so. Very well. We'll review this passage tomorrow and go on. You did well, Fanny. You're dismissed."

The Bible plopped into Fanny's lap. She snatched it up and leaped to her feet. "Thank you, mum." She fled.

Fanny could smell the roses as she entered

her room. She tossed her Bible on the bed and picked up the vase of flowers. She carried them downstairs. They would look much better on the dining room table. She returned to her room and opened the window wide.

Ananias and Sapphira. Daisy and Fanny. The smell of roses lingered.

One white rose—such a small thing.

Fanny would never ever again lie to God!

As soon as she got the nerve, she would go down and confess to Mrs. Hawley, though she was certain Mrs. Hawley knew anyway.

The lesson was supposed to have been in Luke today.

6

Of Coach Horses and Open Windows

November 1834

Graaack! Grgl grlgr grick!

The blue jays were squabbling again. Fanny
leaned her elbows on the sill of the open window
and propped her chin in her hands. She didn't
like the jays to squabble. She didn't like the cats
to catch birds. She didn't like a lot of what went
on in the world. And yet, the world thought she
did. She was like two different people—a cheery,
bright person on the outside and a grumpy, miserable person on the inside. The chill November
rain blipped and pittered inches from her nose,
but she kept the window open anyway. She
wanted to hear outside, even if she didn't like the
jays squabbling. She didn't have many open windows left anymore.

Her dear grandmother had died three years
ago, when Fanny was only eleven. With Grandma
Eunice's passing, one of Fanny's brightest windows on the world went dark. It was Grandma
who had taught Fanny there are many different

kinds of birds, many kinds of trees and flowers. She taught Fanny to tell the differences between them. She showed Fanny how to tell the differences between people, too. She helped Fanny learn whole books of the Bible—and many poems. When Grandma Eunice described something, the picture glowed in Fanny's imagination. It was almost like being able to see. Unfortunately, school was no such window.

Fanny, who so longed for an education, couldn't stand school. She didn't like the schoolmaster telling her she was stupid. She didn't like the way he made her sit still at recess when everyone else ran and played. She didn't like waiting in heavy silence for hours while all the other children read quietly to themselves. But without school, how could she learn anything at all?

She said her umptieth prayer to the heavenly Father for some schooling, but she was beginning to lose confidence. She was fourteen now. All her friends were graduating from eighth grade, most of them finishing their schooling soon. Fanny had not really started yet. Here she was, nearly grown up, and she could not even read or write. People said she composed lovely poems. But unless someone wrote her poems down for her, they were empty, alive only in her mind.

She was even small physically, only half grown up. She could tell because her mother's voice, and most others', came from somewhere above her own head. Strangers who commented on her dark curly hair always sounded surprised when they heard how old she was.

The blue jays flew away, still grousing. Fanny's mother was calling. Fanny hooked the shutters and closed the window. She made her way to the kitchen.

"Fanny." Her mother was sitting by the stove.

"Yes'm?" Fanny heard a piece of paper rattle as she walked to her mother's side.

"The post brought this letter a few minutes ago."

"I heard his horse. What does it say?"

"It's a letter of acceptance from a school in New York. Permission for you to attend there."

Fanny's mouth dropped open. "A—in New York? —a—?"

"It's called the New York Institution for the Blind. It's been operating about three years, they say, and they teach only blind children."

"How can they teach blind people who can't see printing?"

"I have no idea how. It says they do. You may go if you wish."

"For blind people? You're sure?" Fanny's breastbone tickled. Happy surprises always did that to her. "Oh, my. Yes, I—oh, thank God! He answered my prayer, just like I knew He would!"

How could she ever have doubted?

Four months later, on a cold March day a scant three weeks before her fifteenth birthday, Fanny awoke to a whole new day. This was the day she would go to New York. Alone. Was Fanny nervous and worried? The buttons would not button up right on her dress. Her shoes wouldn't go on right. When she ran to the kitchen and plopped down at the table her breakfast stuck in her throat. She couldn't swallow. Her mouth was dry. Her throat was all lumpy, and she couldn't talk well, either.

Her mother undid the buttons and buttoned her dress up correctly. "Oh, Fanny. You're growing up, and yet—how will you manage without me? You've never been away from home for more than a few weeks, and then you were with friends and relatives. Are you sure about this?"

Fanny nodded. "I'm not learning anything here. If they can truly teach me—" She put her spoon down. Trying to eat was useless. "I'll do anything I have to to get an education. And give up anything I have to give up."

Firm, gentle hands squeezed her shoulders. "You'r right, Fan, but still"—Mother's voice shook a little—"I'm glad you have this chance." She didn't sound glad.

Fanny heard the stagecoach coming. Its iron tires clattered in the frozen ruts outside. Even louder was the clop-clop of the horses. Fanny should hug her mother now. She should say something loving and well-spoken. She could not. She hopped up, grabbed her shawl, and ran out the door. The cold air hit her face and tightened up her cheeks. She hurried toward the sound of nervous horses, restless to be on their way.

The horses had been working. Fanny could feel a little aura of warmth; Grandma Eunice once said that hot horses put up clouds of steam on cold days.

"Here ye go, miss." A man's gloved hand took hers. It led her carefully to a—*clunk!* Fanny's knee hit an iron bar. It was a step. She stood on it and took another step. She was inside the coach.

"Right here, dear." A pleasant woman's voice and hand guided her. Fanny sat down on a crackly-stiff cold seat. She bit her lower lip to keep it from trembling. Outside, a horse sneezed.

Her mother's voice said something to the driver. Something *whumped* on the wooden roof above—Fanny's bag, probably. She should say good-bye now. She kept her lip tightly imprisoned in her teeth.

"The window beside you is open," the woman said.

Fanny reached out to her left. Here was the little wooden sill. She extended her hand out farther, into the cold breeze, and waved. The coach rocked from side to side as the driver climbed up into his box. He called out from on high, and the coach lurched forward. Fanny jerked against the leather seat back. She was on her way.

The woman beside her talked, off and on. The lady was going to New York also, she said. She would accompany Fanny all the way, she said. She was happy to, she said. Fanny tried to pay attention to the lady, but she couldn't. Her mind was stuffed with thoughts of home. Mother. Grandma Eunice's grave. Violets in spring and roses in summer.

The coach stopped as they changed horses. Fanny heard the tired horses led away, the new horses harnessed in. Different animals, same clip-clop—they were on their way again.

Fanny thought of all the friends she was leaving behind and all the dogs she greeted as she went walking. There was the butcher's big horse;

Fanny fed it a carrot every time the meat wagon came by. That horse, powerful enough to haul the laden meat wagon up steep hills, was so gentle it tickled Fanny's palm. It was a friend. Fanny thought of autumn and the rich, musty smell of fallen leaves. Crisp and crumbly maple leaves, iron-hard butternuts, those huge horse-chestnuts still in their thick wrappers. Her hands shook.

The woman beside her laid a gloved hand on hers. "Fanny, if you don't want to go to New York we'll get off at the next stop. We can take a return stage back to your home." The hand patted hers. "Besides. Your mother will be lonesome without you."

That did it. All Fanny's dread and longing uncorked at once. Wild, gulping sobs doubled her up as the woman gathered her close. She cried so violently she couldn't breathe.

The warm hand rubbed her heaving shoulder. "There, there, dear. It's no disgrace to love home. We'll be turned around and headed back soon."

Fanny shook her head. She fought the sobs to a standstill. "No." A couple more shuddering sobs jolted her. "No. I'll do better now." Fanny sat up straight. "I'm going to New York. I prayed to God for years and years to send me to school, and now here's a school for people just like me. I mustn't go running home, even if Mother—" She clamped her teeth down again on her lip.

Even as she said that, Fanny smiled to herself. "Talk is cheap," Mrs. Hawley always said. "It's easy to say you'll do something; the mettle is tested when you have to do it." How true. Fanny had one chance to fill up that hideous empty spot inside, if it could be filled at all. And it was up to Fanny herself. She must do it, or not do it, herself.

For years Fanny had talked boldly of wanting an education, of doing anything to get one. But that was just the talk. Now, from this moment on—Fanny Crosby was going to have to do it.

7

Of Meadowlarks and Anna

March 1835

The first warm, wet breezes of spring feel like no other breezes. Autumn might be wet and January unseasonably warm, but spring is spring. Fanny sat in the open carriage as it jostled along rutted streets. She heard the spring mud squish under the wheels. She listened to the horses' hollow feet plop-plopping through the slop. The robins must not be back yet, but two sparrows practiced their scales along the roadside.

A whiff of unfettered wind told her the countryside had opened up. They were passing through fields. The open feeling closed down. There must be a woodlot to windward. Yes—Fanny could smell that faint odor unique to second-growth trees with the sap rising. Grandma Eunice had explained about sap every year at sugaring time.

"How far are we going?" Fanny asked.

The driver called back from his box above her. "Your school is way out on Ninth Avenue. That's six blocks from the nearest stage stop. That's why your friends sent you out from the city in this carriage; saves you walking through this muck. You're nearly at the end of your journey. How has it been?"

"Very nice, thank you. My mother brought me to New York once when I was five, you know."

"Eh? Things've changed some since, I aver."

Fanny smiled. "Yes. The first time took days in a farm wagon and then a schooner. This time I came in a coach and a river steamer."

"Big improvement, aye?" The coachman stopped his team. A heavy coach of some sort clattered by in front of them.

"I suppose. The trip is faster now, especially the coach part. But schooners—well, they smell good, like old friends. The steamboat smelled like a fire in a wet woodlot. And schooners' decks tilt when they change tack. The steamer stayed so level you might as well be home. But the sea gulls were the same." She laughed. "I'm sure they're exactly what they've always been. Noisy old sea gulls."

The seat creaked up there. His voice pointed Fanny's way now. "Y'know, Miss; talking to you, I can see that we who have our sight miss most of what's going on around us. We don't even notice the feel and smell and sound of things. Just how much do you 'see,' so to speak?" He turned back forward and clucked to his team.

"Well—your near horse—the one on the left—tends to be a little lazy. You're constantly flicking the whip his way. They are both rather large as carriage horses go (from the sound of their large feet in the mud), but you probably like them large because you yourself are a large man—the way your seat creaks there."

The fellow laughed. "You're right, right down the line."

"I hear a meadowlark off to the left, which means more open fields. Larks never sing in the woods. And we just passed a crossroad. The ruts bumped opposite the wheels."

"Amazing. Nothing short of amazing. Well, Miss, here you are."

The coach rolled to a squishy stop. Fanny had no idea just what she expected, but somehow this wasn't it. She sat out in the middle of mud and damp breeze, nowhere near the bustling town. She heard no children laughing or reciting or anything. She felt incredibly exposed and alone, the only person in a dull and vacant world.

"Frances Crosby?" A charming Quaker lady's voice spoke from the right. "Welcome to our school."

"Thank you, Mum." Fanny stood up and turned right. A soft, pudgy hand took hers and helped her down the step. Fanny's bags splacked in the wet. Someone other than the lady picked them up. The footsteps sounded like a man's.

The coachman called a cheery good-bye. The wheels splashed past Fanny and swung into a wide turn in the roadway. She listened to the horses, to their broad feet and heavy breathing. The carriage sounds dissolved into the distance; her last link with the world she knew dissolved with them. She stood stranded in a vast, empty world; a cold, dull, unfamiliar world, uncaring, unfriendly.

"Come along, Frances." The warm hand laid itself across Fanny's shoulders and pressed her forward. They walked through quiet emptiness.

"Does thy mother call thee Frances?"

"No'm. Fanny." The slop soaked clear through her shoes.

"Then will I. Steps here, Fanny."

Fanny groped ahead with a toe. Three stone steps into the building. Without really thinking about it, Fanny logged the numbers in her memory for future reference. They walked along cool, silent halls—silent except for the *squish squish* of Fanny's shoes. Her toes were so cold they hurt.

Where was everybody? She remembered the long hours of painful silence as she sat in the school back home. Now there would be days and weeks and months of that kind of torture—and no way for a blind girl to escape and go home. Whatever had she got herself into this time? She wanted to be home. She wanted her mother. She wanted to sit in a kitchen with warm and homey smells. She wanted to lie in her familiar bed and listen to the great horned owls hoot, to hear the rain drip behind the shutters. Fanny snuffled. Her nose started running.

"Upstairs." The lady turned Fanny aside and put her hand on a rail. Thirteen steps, a landing, fourteen steps. "Third door left, Fanny." The lady extended Fanny's left hand so that her fingers touched the wall. She brushed past a door frame. One—another—two— "Here we are. This is thy room, Fanny. I trust it pleases thee."

The dooor opened, and Fanny stepped inside.

"Her" room. It didn't smell like her room. It was much colder than her room. Was it furnished? With what? If it were her room she would know those things. The person carrying her bags plopped them down nearby. His footsteps left.

Here came the sobbing again. She covered

her face with her hands. Her crying embarrassed her for only a moment. Then she didn't care what the cold world thought of her.

The warm hands pulled her in tight against an ample, cushiony bosom. "Ah, Fanny, I guess thee has never been away from home before."

"No'm." Her sobbing kept breaking up what she wanted to say. "Not this—this far."

" 'Twill take some getting used to. 'Tis the same with all the new pupils. Hark! They're coming back from their walk outside. Soon thee will not be feeling quite so lonely."

A babbling gaggle of children's voices filled the hallway outside Fanny's doorway. A booming voice of authority gave orders. The cacophony came pouring down the hall this way.

"Dr. Russ!" the lady called. "Our new girl here, Frances Jane Crosby. She prefers Fanny to Frances. Fanny, this is Dr. Russ, our superintendent." The lady stepped back.

A huge paw grasped Fanny's right hand and shook it, very grown-up-like. "How do you do, Miss Crosby, and welcome." The paw released her, the voice pointed away. "Anna! Anna, come in here, please."

A girl's light, melodic voice answered from the doorway. "Yes, Dr. Russ?"

"Frances Crosby here. Call her Fanny. I leave it to you to help her feel comfortable." The paw patted Fanny's shoulder. "We'll talk again soon, Miss Crosby." She heard him leave.

"I must tend to others now." The lady stuffed a dry hankie into Fanny's hand. "Lift thy spirits. Thee will feel better soon."

Fanny wiped her face and blew, alone again.

"Am I glad you blew your nose! I was having

trouble finding you." The girl's voice was right next to her. A cool hand touched her arm and took her own hand. "Come sit on the footlockers. We'll talk. You can unpack later."

Fanny followed obediently. "You're blind, too?"

"We all are, except some of the adults. Now let's—" Brass rattled. "This is Audrey's bed. The footrail is loose; hear it? That means your bed is right here" (her hand rapped on wood) "and each bed has a foot locker. There. Got it?"

Fanny groped a little and sat down on an enameled wooden chest with brass corners. "How many people live in this room?"

"Four at the moment. And if another signs up, five. They just keep moving beds in. I suppose someday the room will be a single vast bed from wall to wall. But I don't know where they'd put the washstands then. Funny. The washstands just sit there nearly all day, taking up space and being idle. But when you want one everyone wants one. So there are never enough wash- stands when you need them and there are too many when you don't. How old are you?"

"I'll be fifteen in two weeks."

"Go to school anywhere before?"

"No, not really." Fanny took a deep breath. The sobs seemed done.

"So what's your favorite thing to do?" Anna's voice was eye-level to Fanny. She must be sit- ting on a footlocker also.

Fanny was about to mention how much she enjoyed writing poetry. She thought a moment. "When I was very small, I used to sneak rides on the neighbors' horses. And then when I was older, I'd go out riding with others. I've always liked riding horses."

"Why?"

Fanny had to think. "I suppose it's because you have all the power under control—well, most of the time it's under control. Horses are interesting anyway—each one is unique, with a personality all its own. And yet, after you ride a horse awhile something clicks and the two of you are—well, together. And I like writing poetry, too."

"Controlling words instead of horses. Making words do what you want them to."

Fanny grinned suddenly. "Anna, I thank God you're here. I think we're going to be special. What's your favorites?"

"Me?" She laughed. "I like everything most, I guess. Schoolwork, and figuring out why people think the way they do, and learning. You'll study arithmetic here, and English and grammar, science, astronomy, history, and philosophy. And political science. Oh, and music."

"Not poetry?"

"Plenty of poetry. Dr. Russ just loves poetry, so we get lots of it. He spends hours reading to us. He knew Lord Byron personally when he was over in Greece. You know, Byron? *Prisoner of Chillon* Byron?"

"Yes, I heard of Byron—and not a single nice word about him. You should hear what our Methodist minister said about him—immoral, wild, profligate. And Dr. Russ *knows* him?"

"Knew him. He died, you know. Now here's how you take your lessons. First the teacher reads the lesson. Then he or she asks you questions. And the next day you recite that lesson all back again before you start the next one. And music, of course, is singing and instruments."

"I play the guitar—fairly well, I'm told."

"Too bad."

"What?" Fanny frowned. Most people looked on her guitar playing favorably.

"Guitar fingers. The tips of your fingers are toughened up. You see, Dr. Russ developed this way to read by touch with embossed letters. Raised letters. They're hard to feel if your fingers are calloused. But don't worry about it," Anna went on hastily. "You'll get on fine here."

They sat on the footlockers and kicked their feet and talked and talked. Other girls came and went. Eventually Fanny met just about everyone. Her homesickness simmered down. It would boil up again, now and then, in the weeks that followed. But from that first afternoon, chatting with Anna, Fanny could feel a change in herself—a growth.

This was home.

8

Of Melons and the Dark of Night

Late Summer 1838

Fanny finished the last of her mashed potatoes and gravy and laid her fork across her plate. She reached across and tapped her finger on the table. "You. Amelia. You haven't spoken a word the whole meal. Eating fast or feeling low?"

Amelia giggled, a sad little titter. "Very sensitive you are. I'm feeling low. You must be Fanny Crosby."

"You have a good ear for voices."

She tittered again. "I don't need a good ear. It's your reputation. 'Fanny says whatever comes to her mind—and plenty comes.'"

Fanny poked Anna beside her. "Do you hear that, Anna? My reputation! Honestly. Well, I know just how you feel, Amelia, because I, too, felt low my first few months here. It passes, though. Soon this place will feel like home."

"You've been here how long? Four years?"

"Three years," Fanny replied. "And I've loved every minute of it. Except for the hideous monster, of course."

Amelia gasped. "You're not talking about the new superintendent, I hope."

"Oh, my, no. Arithmetic."

Anna cut in, "Fanny and arithmetic is like Crusaders and Turks. She had a terrible time. Despised it. I tried to tutor her, splendid mathematician that I am, but you can't teach a stone long division. Dr. Russ finally excused her from arithmetic. You should have heard her. She didn't just stumble through her multiplication tables; she fell all over them."

Amelia was giggling, and it was not such a sad titter anymore.

Fanny wiped her sweaty face with her napkin; she'd forgotten her hankie again. She tucked the napkin in its ring. "This heat. Summer is lovely for the birds and flowers, but the heat! Ah, at least it ripens the melons nicely. Have you been out visiting the melon patch yet, Amelia? They planted the whole school field in melons this year. The melons must be this big by now." She tapped the table with both hands held two feet apart.

"You're counting chickens that will never hatch," Anna's fork clunked on her plate. "They intend to sell every single one of those melons. Profit. All profit. We don't get a nibble."

"Surely not! Why, that would be dastardly! So many lovely melons and not a one for us?"

Anna sniffed. "I suppose they need the money more than they need sticky seeds and melon sugar smeared all over the school."

Fanny got a wildly wicked idea—just the thing to cure young Amelia's homesickness. "Amelia, dear child, how old are you?"

"Thirteen."

"And I am eighteen. Therefore you must look upon me as your sage elder counselor. Come with me, please."

Anna hooted. "Fanny is a sage elder, and I'm the Empress Josephine! Enjoy her lovely poetry, Amelia, but don't you dare believe a single word she says. I'm going to practice my music. Good evening, ladies." Anna's chair scraped against the wooden floor.

Amelia was laughing. Good! The anti-home-sickness tonic was working.

Fanny stood up. "You must show me where you sleep." She tucked her own chair under the table. "I shall come for you tonight, and we'll become heroes together." She chatted with Amelia all the way to the girl's room, but in the back of her mind Fanny was plotting one of her most daring pranks ever.

Pranks? Ah, yes. Fanny prided herself on the clever gags and pranks she pulled. After all, what would life be if everyone sat around all sober and stuffy? There was, however, one big problem. Whenever a particularly wild and devastating prank was pulled, Fanny got blamed whether it was hers or not. Some ingenious trickster—and probably several of them—was getting away scot-free at Fanny's expense!

The evening wore on slowly. Fanny practiced her music. She carefully rehearsed in her mind everything they would do, and where, and when. She pretended to prepare for bed, but she kept her clothes on, all but her shoes. She would need bare feet for this, so that she might feel at all times exactly where she was. It must look strange on a hot night like tonight that Fanny should tuck the covers up around her chin.

The school fell silent. Fanny listened to the matron's footfalls as the lady checked each bed, counted each head. The footsteps clicked away down the hall.

Fanny got up. She moved to the door and listened. She slipped out into the hall and hurried downstairs. Here was Amelia's bed, the second one over. Fanny felt her way to the pillow and tapped softly.

"Wh—?"

Fanny whispered, "Are you dressed and ready?"

"Yes," Amelia hissed. She connected with Fanny's hand. Together they tiptoed into the hall. Fanny led, for she knew her way intimately, and Amelia still groped a lot. They hurried down to the kitchen door.

Fanny slipped a spoon handle through the hinge side so the door stayed open a crack. The girls sneaked outside, listening with every step. The warm air of a late-summer night flowed around Fanny's face as she hurried to the back garden gate. Now they had left the yard. And now they were walking the length of the hedge-row beside the melon field.

Fanny whispered, "I can taste the melon already."

"I'm not sure I want to do this. It's scary."

"Of course it's scary. Anything heroic includes an element of danger. St. George didn't slay the dragon with the dragon's mouth tied shut. You do want to be a hero, don't you?"

"I don't think so."

They paused again to listen. What was that? Footsteps coming! Fortunately, the moon would not come up for another hour yet, at least. Whoever the person was, he or she probably could not see much better than Fanny could.

Fanny pushed Amelia down to the ground. "Squirm under the hedge there. Don't move. Don't make a sound. Listen and wait. I shall return promptly." She could tell by the sound of Amelia's breathing that the child was terrified. Perhaps this had not been such a glorious idea after all. The hedge rattled. Amelia was secure.

From the distance came Mr. Stephen's voice— Mr. Stephens, the gardener. "Halt! Who goes there?"

Fanny started toward him. "Why, Mr. Stephens, good evening. You're certainly out late. How can you pull weeds in the darkness?" She laughed. "Just listen to me! That's the same sort of silly question we get all the time from sighted visitors. Did you hear what Robert told that woman visitor this afternoon?"

Mr. Stephens was close now. "Ah, it's you, Fanny. No. What did Robert say?"

"The woman asked him how he managed to find his mouth with his fork when he ate, as if sight had anything to do with it. So he says, 'Why, we tie one end of a string to our chair leg and the other end to our tongue. Then we just follow the string.'"

Mr. Stephens laughed. "That's Robert, all right. Or you, young lady—something you'd say. What are you doing out here so late?"

"It's so hot I can't sleep. I was hoping cool night air would make me drowsy. But why are you out here, Mr. Stephens?"

"I'm watching for some miserable boys that's trying to steal our melons. Imagine, stealing from the blind. I'll catch the rascals yet. Didn't happen to hear anyone during your ramblings, did you, Fanny?"

"No, not a rustle." This was perfect! This was better than her wildest plotting. Fanny adjusted her voice carefully. She must sound both concerned and casual. "You sound tired, Mr. Stephens. You know, until the moon comes up I can watch as well as you. Why don't you sit down and rest a few minutes? I'll stay out here and keep my ears tuned. Sit. Relax. I can't sleep anyway."

"No, I couldn't—" His voice trailed off. "Of course, in this darkness you can watch better than I, for your ears are far sharper than mine. But I hate to ask that of you, Fanny."

"You're not asking. I did. I'm more than happy to." Fanny took his arm and headed toward the gardener's cottage. "Not long. A quarter hour's rest will perk you up. And you may depend on it: if a single boy comes around, I'll let you know."

"Just yell loud, and I'll come running." He paused. "I really shouldn't—"

Fanny pressed on. "Here we are. I'll call you in a quarter hour, I promise. You needn't feel guilty. I've a pretty good clock inside my head."

He chuckled. "You've a pretty good head all around. And a sweet and thoughtful child you are, too. I'll leave the door open here, so I can hear you." He stepped inside.

Fanny waited at the door, listening until Mr. Stephen's chair creaked.

Quickly she hurried back along the hedgerow, the soft tilled dirt under her feet. "Amelia," she whispered. "Amelia? You may come out now."

The bushes rattled just ahead. Fanny made her way quickly to the noise. "Now let's choose the perfect melon."

Amelia kept her voice low, but it had regained its firm feel of confidence. "I'm very good at picking ripe ones. Uncle Nick says I have an ear for it." She thumped from melon to melon. "These all belong to the school, don't they?"

"Every one of them."

"And we're part of the school, are we not?" Amelia thumped another melon.

"More than just a part. We're the whole reason for the school. You might say we and the school are one." Fanny felt quite philosophical.

"Then it's not stealing."

"Absolutely not. If we were those boys Mr. Stephens mentioned, we would be stealing, for the melons would not belong to us. This, Amelia, is appropriation. Nothing more. After all, we've been eating fruit and vegetables all summer from these fields and gardens."

"And putting up vegetables for winter use. I'm so tired of waxing turnips."

"Not as tired as you'll be of eating them next winter. How's this one?" Fanny rapped what must be the biggest melon in the patch.

"Sounds good." Amelia thumped it. She thumped it again. "Splendid. I guarantee this is the reddest, juiciest—"

Fanny grabbed the prickly stem in both hands and wrenched it free. She hefted the melon. "It's bigger than you are, Amelia. Come along quickly." She carried the melon to the back gate. "Take it to our room and summon the other girls. I'll be there in fifteen minutes. I'll bring the carving knife."

Amelia giggled. "Anna might be the Empress Josephine, but you are Napoleon. Bold, decisive—

and sneaky!" She hurried off to the house with
their prize.

Fanny hung around the far end of the patch,
listening. No boys. She made a complete circuit,
down the far hedgerow and past the fruit trees
to the cottage. She marked the march of minutes.
It was time. She paused at the door only a
moment, listening to the deep, sonorous breathing. "Mr. Stephens. Mr. Stephens?"

He snuffled. He snorted. "What? Fanny." The
chair creaked. He came to the door. "Did you
hear anything?"

Fanny said in absolute truth, "Not a boy has
been by, sir."

"Mm. Good. Good. I feel much refreshed."

"Even the nighthawks have gone to bed, and
so shall I. I'm sure I'll sleep well now. Thank
you, Mr. Stephens."

"Why, thank *you*, Fanny. Good night."

"Good night." Fanny made her way back up
the hedgerow, following the plow line with her
bare feet. She walked through the scratchy weeds
to the gate; her conscience hardly pricked at all.
She squeezed through the gate and ran to the
kitchen door. She slipped inside, put the spoon
away, and chose a long sharp knife.

Fanny flew upstairs, listening only a moment
for footsteps in the halls. All was clear. She
hurried to the room. "It's me," she whispered.

"She's back! It's time!" A chorus of happy whis-
pers surrounded her.

Fanny worked her way through the sea of night-
gowns to the footlocker. Here was the melon, as
big as the footlocker and even more tempting
than when it lay in the field. Fanny thumped it
triumphantly.

She paused a moment before cutting into it. Fanny Crosby had just pulled off a prank most sighted people could never manage. She had done it with smoothness, aplomb, polish. She orchestrated Amelia through prior planning and Mr. Stephens instinctively. She had performed the caper herself, on her own.

Her only regret—the only thing wrong with her coup—was that such a magnificent prank did nothing toward filling up that empty spot. Impatiently, she pushed the thought aside.

Fanny sliced down through the delectable melon. "Let the feast begin!"

9

Of Skull Bumps and Poetry

Fall 1839

Fanny hurried along the corridor to the super-intendent's office, humming the new tune she heard yesterday.

"Hi, Fanny!"

She recognized the voice. "Hello, Lester."

"That poem you wrote about the teachers sure was great! So was the one at the dedication."

"Thank you, Lester."

"You're the best poet in the world. Everybody says so."

"That's very flattering. Thank you." Fanny smiled as she continued on her way. All the students who talked to her just loved her poems, it seemed. Her teachers might be rather cool toward her poetry; on the other hand, they kept asking her for poems for special occasions and excursions.

Dr. Russ had gone on to other things. For these last three years Mr. Silas Jones had been superintendent. He was a nice enough man. He praised Fanny's poetry now and then, and he seemed genuinely concerned for the students.

He had summoned Fanny today. What did he want? Sometimes he asked her to write a poem specifically for some occasion; perhaps that would be the case today. Or perhaps he wanted to tell her he liked that poem she delivered at the cornerstone dedication of the new school building. Everyone else had praised it.

Fanny tapped at Mr. Jones's office door. He mumbled.

She stuck her head inside the door. "Fanny Crosby, sir. You asked me to come after breakfast. Is this a good time?"

"Fine. Come in, Fanny. Be seated."

Mr. Jones's office must have a large window. Compared with the dank hall, it was sunshine warm. She crossed until she bumped into a big leather chair. She was not very familiar with this room. She perched in the chair, her feet barely touching the floor. She might be twenty years old now, but she was still too short to fit in chairs comfortably.

Mr. Jones sat silent a few moments. "It has come to my attention—" He cleared his throat. "Fanny, I'm sorry that you've let yourself be carried away by what others say about your verses."

She frowned. "Sir?"

"It's true that you've written a number of poems of real merit. But—"

"Thank you, sir." Ah. He was going to praise her efforts.

"*But!* They fall far short of the excellence you might attain. Briefly spoken, Fanny, you are doing well, but you could do much better. You've let flattering words lull you into complacency. You know what complacency means?"

"Uh, satisfied with things as they are, one might say."

"Even better, self-satisfied. Satisfied with your self as you are. That's fatal. You'll never stretch and grow and improve if you believe the flattering remarks of your fellow pupils."

Flattering. Fanny herself had used that word just moments ago.

Mr. Jones continued. "Avoid a flatterer as you would avoid a poisonous snake, Fanny. No true friend would deceive you by flattery. And remember this: Whatever talent you possess is not from your own self. It comes from God and belongs to God. You ought give Him the credit for everything you achieve."

"Yes, sir," she mumbled. This was nothing at all as she had expected when she walked in.

"Now, let us talk about the practical routes to improvement. First, your talent is raw. Undisciplined. You must smooth and polish your verses; rework them as needed so they may be of more value. Secondly, store up as much useful knowledge in your mind as you can. You will call upon every scrap of it sooner or later. You are making progress already, but you must work, Fanny! Then you'll attain the goal of being a fine poetess."

Fanny mumbled something. She hadn't expected any of this.

His voice softened. "Fanny, have I hurt your feelings too much?"

She was sorely tempted to say yes. It would be the truth. But Mr. Jones also spoke the truth, even if she didn't like it. And his was by far the greater truth, the more important truth. She sat up straight and squared her shoulders. "No, sir. You have talked to me like a father. You've said things I must hear that no one else has said. I thank you very much for it."

"You're a gracious young lady. Thank you, Fanny. You're excused now."

She stood again and curtsied in the direction of his voice. "Thank you again, Mr. Jones." She heard his chair squeak as he stood up. His hand led her to the door.

"Good day, Fanny."

Suddenly she was standing out in the cool hall all alone.

"Good morning, Fanny." That was Miss Hulsmeyer, all businesslike. She brushed past Fanny and swept in through Mr. Jones's door. The warm air came pouring out around Fanny.

"I have a number of things to discuss," Miss Hulsmeyer was saying, "and one of them is that child outside your door. We've been—" The door clicked shut.

It is impolite to listen in on others' conversations. But this conversation was obviously about Fanny herself. She backed up to the door and leaned casually against the wall, her ear to the crack.

". . . consensus of the faculty that she spends so much time with her poetry so-called that she's neglecting her studies. She is attending this school to learn, not muse. Oh, I've done my part, believe me. I've warned her about hampering her education. I've confiscated her poems. I've forbidden her from writing. But she ignores me. Disobedience is what we're talking about here, Mr. Jones. Flagrant disobedience."

"Well, ah, Miss Hulsmeyer—"

"Mr. Jones, you are well aware that there's no end of would-be poets. They're common as dirt and about as interesting. A penny the cartload. We do her a disservice to let her think she might someday be a poet of superior caliber."

"Miss Hulsmeyer, I doubt she'll be discouraged so easily. You yourself say you've tried and failed."

"The word must come from you. Threaten her with expulsion. Do what you must."

"Expel a good student because she writes poetry? Come now, Miss Hulsmeyer."

"But she is hindering her own progress with this obsession for spinning doggerel. We all agree."

"If it's the opinion of all concerned, I suppose—" His chair squeaked. "Tell you what, Miss Hulsmeyer. Let's see how much her poetry-writing actually affects her grades. I'll forbid her to write poetry for—oh, let's see—three months. There should be a light at the end of her tunnel. No poetry for three months. Not a word, not a line. We'll see how much better her work is and whether she can improve her studies and be a poet at the same time. We'll work something out. And now what's next on your list?"

"About Robert—"

Fanny pushed away from the wall and started down the hall, numb. Three months! Three whole months! To not think up lovely rhymes and words for a whole fourth of a year—surely Mr. Jones didn't mean it. Surely he was only mollifying the harsh Miss Hulsmeyer.

No. Fanny knew that wasn't so. Mr. Jones was an honest man. He would never say something to Miss Hulsmeyer or anyone else unless he meant every word of it. Three whole months! Very well, she would begin right now. She would pay very careful attention in class. She would rehearse her lessons in her head every night.

She would study her music with greater care
and gusto. She would learn every word taught
her, precept on precept, line on line, here a bit
and there a bit, as the Scripture said. Where
was that? Isaiah somewhere. You see? She was
already amassing useful knowledge (of course,
she had learned that particular bit from Grandma
Eunice years ago). Her intentions were noble,
her desire to please Mr. Jones sincere. Her greatest goal was to achieve an education, and she
had already said she would give up anything she
had to do it.

So why were there tears in her eyes?

A month passed. Two more weeks plodded
by. Oh, my, the time dragged slowly! Now, on a
sunny Monday morning, Fanny sat poking at
her cornmeal mush with a spoon. She didn't feel
like eating. She never felt like eating lately.

Someone tapped her arm. A smiling tenor voice
lilted, "Good morning, Fanny!"

"Good morning, Dr. Reiff." Fanny smiled even
if she didn't feel very happy. Everyone loved Dr.
Reiff—he cared so much about his pupils. He
was an excellent singing instructor, too.

"Mr. Jones asked me to tell you: he wishes to
see you in his office after breakfast."

"Thank you, Dr. Reiff." The ray of sunshine
faded as the teacher walked away. Fanny made
a few more idle stabs at her breakfast and pushed
the dish away. She might as well go get this over
with. She knew her grades were poor. Now she'd
never again get to write poetry. They'd keep
restricting her more and more, and then her
grades would fall and fall, and—she pushed in
her chair and made her way out.

The hallway was as clammy as ever. Someone wished her good morning, and she replied. Again, she was being cheery on the outside and miserable inside. In a way, she was a living, walking lie. She knocked at the superintendent's office and was invited in.

"Ah, Fanny. Come sit down, please."

She slipped from clammy cool into sunshine warm and closed the door behind her.

His chair squeaked. "You've lost a little weight. Been eating well enough?"

"Sufficient, thank you, sir."

"Do you feel ill? Aches, pains, malaise?"

"No, sir. My health is good enough, thank you, sir."

"Then what's the trouble with your schoolwork?" He sounded impatient. "Your teachers report your grades have slipped disastrously since last term. If not illness, what is it?"

She lifted her shoulders and let them fall. "I'm sorry, sir. I tried. I truly tried. But I find it impossible to concentrate on studies. All I can think about is writing poetry—more specifically, not writing poetry, which is my present circumstance. Poetry is all I think about. I can't help it." She sighed and muttered, "I'm sorry," again. She really was sorry, too.

Mr. Jones grunted thoughtfully. "Obviously, our little experiment isn't working. So much for science. Very well, Fanny. That business about abstaining from poetry for three months is ended. Over. I rescind the edict. You may write poetry as much as you wish. However"—he bellowed the word—"I expect you to pay better attention to your lectures. Apply yourself more. I expect significant improvement in your marks, understand?"

Fanny's grin pushed her cheeks so wide apart they hurt. "Oh, Mr. Jones! I'll do so much better. I mean," she corrected herself, "I shall try to do better. No, I'll do more than try. I shall accomplish."

Mr. Jones laughed. "The little lady who will do it all herself. Very well, Fanny. You're dismissed. Oh, and incidentally, we're having a visitor shortly, a phrenologist. Do you know what a phrenologist is?"

"I know *ology* is the study or knowledge of, but I don't know the *phren*."

"The mind. Specifically, studying the outside of the skull to determine special gifts and skills inside the mind. It should be interesting to hear what he has to say about you. Good day, Fanny."

"Good day. And thank you, sir! Thank you!" Fanny bounced out the door like a spring lamb.

A rough wool dress brushed past her. "Good morning, Frances."

"Good morning, Miss Hulsmeyer."

"You wished to see me?" Hiss Hulsmeyer was closing the office door.

"Yes. About Fanny. Our experiment to curb her poetry-writing seems to have foundered on the rocks of melancholy. I've given her permission to take up her poetry again. I ask that you and the other teachers not discourage her in any way. Let's see if we can jack her scholarship back up to its former aptness."

Fanny heard Miss Hulsmeyer fretting, but she didn't catch the words. She whistled away down the hall, suddenly as happy as the bobbing robins out on the yard.

Sure enough, just as Mr. Jones promised, a widely noted phrenologist came to the school.

Famous visitors, and many not-so-famous people, came through the New York Institution for the Blind. Apparently the school was one of the best, and one of the few, to serve the handicapped. It was considered one of those stops one ought to make when passing through New York City. Fanny was not especially excited, therefore, that this was a man well-known on two continents. What did excite her was the mystery of phrenology.

The students were gathered together. From the front of the room Mr. Jones introduced the man with that deep droning tone of voice he saved for important guests.

"Pupils, we have with us today Dr. George Combe. Dr. Combe was born and educated in Edinburgh, Scotland (am I correct in that, doctor?). Yes. Some years ago he traveled to Paris and there learned the science of phrenology. He is now considered one of the world's foremost authorities in this science. He founded the phrenological society in this country and also its journal. He is an eminent scientist, and we are honored that he is visiting us today. Without further ado, here is Dr. Combe."

Fanny loved Dr. Combe's voice. It rumbled. It sang. A strong Scots brogue made the edges of its words rough; the *r*'s vibrated. And yet, there was a twinge of English accent about it also. The doctor explained that he was testing the way blindness changes a person's physiognomy. Fanny had no idea what *physiognomy* meant. He praised the fine array of pupils before him. Fanny smiled as she remembered Mr. Jones's warning about flatterers. Dr. Combe's voice moved to this side of the room, near Fanny.

Silence. Miss Hulsmeyer introduced him to Robert on the end bench. Robert said, "How-de-do," and made a muffled noise. Mr. Jones said something reassuring. More silence. What was happening?

"I find no physical evidence of blindness," the doctor rumbled. "How long have you been blind, Robert?"

"Three years, sir."

"Ah. That would explain it. Like history and political science, do you?"

"Yes, sir."

Miss Hulsmeyer gasped in admiration. "Those are indeed his strongest subjects, even his only strong subjects. This is Joan."

What was going on here?

Dr. Combe purred, "Interesting. Interesting." Now he had stepped up to the boy right next to Fanny. "Why here is a splendid mathematician!" the doctor cried. "Remarkably well developed in the area of calculation and pure geometry. Some day you'll hear from him."

"You're so right, doctor!" Miss Hulsmeyer bubbled. "The lad is a mathematical prodigy. I'm amazed, simply amazed. And this next pupil is Fanny."

Dr. Combe hovered over her, his fingers pressed against her head. So this is what he'd been doing to everyone. The fingers probed every inch of her skull, brushing gently, pushing. She sat firm and waited. Could he really read her skull?

"Why, here is a poetess! Remarkable. Give her every advantage she can have. Let her hear the best books. Introduce her to the best writers. She will make her mark in the world."

Miss Hulsmeyer mumbled something grudging, and they moved on.

A poetess. The phrenologist read the little bumps on her head (she didn't know she had any!) and declared what Fanny had known all along. Perhaps now the teachers would not be so impatient with her efforts at poetry. Perhaps now that she would be encouraged and recognized a little more, that little empty spot inside would fill up.

10

Of Fanny Crosby and the Light

November 1850

Progress, they called it. When Fanny Crosby first arrived at the school fifteen years ago, she rode in a borrowed carriage, for there was no public transportation. She had to slog through shifting mud to reach the door. Now here she was, sitting in a fine public horse cab. Most of the streets were paved or cobbled. The old melon field now grew stately two-story houses. Farther into town the buildings crowded wall-to-wall with no space in between.

The cab's wheels hit a rut or hole on the right side. Fanny jolted straight up and came down a few inches over. She was thirty years old now, and her feet still did not touch the floor squarely. True progress would come when they started building these public cabs with a good, gentle suspension system!

The cab bounded off another bump; the younger pupils laughed and whooped. The older people simply said "excuse me" to each other as they collided. Fanny was one of the older people now and for the last three years a teacher, but she whooped anyway.

Being a teacher was much finer than being a pupil. Pupils either learned, or they didn't learn; and frequently a pupil's progress depended upon the teacher. It was the teacher who most often could make the difference between learning and not learning. A teacher could inspire or depress, cheer or discourage. And who knew the needs of blind pupils better than a blind teacher who had just come through the system?

Still—and this was a curious thing—even though Fanny was now doing everything she loved best in the world, that empty place inside was not yet filled. The restless incomplete feeling persisted. Fanny was teaching. She was writing poetry and even articles for papers. Magazines published her work. Six years ago she had published a fine book of poems, *The Blind Girl and Other Poems.* Few sighted people accomplished such things. Fanny Crosby had done all that, all by herself, in thirty years! Daily, pupils thanked her for lectures and her understanding. Visits from presidents and international dignitaries didn't impress her.

She was even establishing an excellent business relationship with the famous composer George Root. He wrote the music, and she supplied the lyrics, and their popular songs were sung all over the country. Her life was full of the finest things possible. Why wasn't all that enough?

"Here you are, folks!" the driver called. "Thirtieth Street Methodist Church." He hesitated. "I thought you folks from the school went to the Eighteenth Street Methodist."

"We usually do," Fanny called as she hopped

down. "But the revival meetings are being held here, not there, so here we are. Thank you, young man, and good night."

"Good night to you, folks."

From the other side of the group, Alice called, "We're all here, Fanny." Alice was sighted; she could count noses. When Fanny chaperoned she could only count voices (and much too frequently the impish children would stand quite silent just to tease her). "Stay together, now, group."

A strong young male hand took Fanny's. "We have seats for you right here, near the middle where the sound is best. No echo. You're from the blind school, right?"

"That's right, and we appreciate your extra attention. You're a fine church!" Fanny gripped the hand and let herself be led.

The young man laughed. "Ah, but I'm such a new member of the church. Why, when I first came to these revival meetings I came to heckle. Foolish man I was! But praise God, He looked past my ignorance and lifted me up. I belong to the Savior now."

"I rejoice for you!" Fanny patted the helpful hand. It left her. She felt around behind for the bench and sat down.

Alice plunked down beside her. "I'll go up with you tonight, Fanny, if you like, when they give the altar call."

"You're a dear, Alice." Fanny patted the shoulder that brushed her own. Somewhere up front, the revivalist's assistant was opening with prayer.

Fanny bowed her head, but her mind was far from the prayer up front. This was the last of the meetings. Twice now Fanny had answered the call to the altar, leaning on the arms of her friends. Nothing had happened either time. Fanny carried her heavy load of emptiness (how heavy emptiness can be!) to the front, and both times she carried it back again to her pew. Tonight, it was now or never. Tonight, either the Lord would lift her up, or she would be ever weighed down by that burden of—of—nothing.

The congregation sang songs. Fanny knew them all by heart. Songs and hymns were a form of poetry she loved best, joyous weddings of words and music. Then the revivalist's assistant asked for donations.

An earnest voice on the aisle called, "You folks from the blind school aren't expected to contribute. You're our guests, and welcome."

Fanny and Alice both acknowledged him, but Fanny's smile felt as hollow as her soul. More songs. More prayer.

The revivalist, now a familiar voice, began speaking. Fanny listened carefully for some key word, for some new explanation that would open some spiritual door. She had heard it all before, many times. The evangelist said it was for the supreme Judge to decide what is sin and what is not. He outlined exactly what sin was in His Word. Then He established the penalty—death. One could pay with one's own death, or one could pay with Jesus Christ's death. In order to accept Jesus's death for his own, the repentant sinner must actively accept God's plan. And then, the sinner was saved not by his own efforts but by God's. His role was to accept it.

The sonorous voice did provide Fanny with good definitions for vague terms she'd heard—and been using herself—for years. "Mercy" was less punishment than you deserve. "Grace" was more blessing than you deserve. Fanny liked the simplicity of that.

The speaker ended with a magnificent flourish of rhetoric. He called all who would repent and accept Jesus to come forward. The meeting was coming to a close.

Alice had offered to come, but Fanny slipped out into the aisle alone. She needed no guiding arm; the flow of people carried her along.

Behind her the congregation began singing a hymn, "At the Cross." Fanny knew this hymn, too. Isaac Watts had written the words long ago. Ralph Hudson had written the music for this particular version. Fanny thought about phrases in the chorus. "At the cross where I first saw the light"—Fanny could barely see light and darkness. She had never experienced the sight of true unfiltered brilliance. "Burden of my heart"—she had that, all right! "I received my sight"—this was written by a sighted man. Therefore, the meaning was obviously spiritual sight. How Fanny yearned for that; she didn't have either kind of sight. "Happy all the day" the song ended. Fanny was happy on the outside, but that was an act. Isaac Watts was not writing here about false fronts.

They sang verses two and three. The song was nearly done, for here was verse four.

> But drops of grief can ne'er repay
> The debt of love I owe:
> Here, Lord, I give myself away,
> 'Tis all that I can do.

She stopped. She gasped. Of course! All these years she wanted to have God's grace Fanny's way. She wanted to follow the world's way. Most of all she wanted to do it herself, just as she had done everything herself, her whole life long. She hated it when other people had to help her. She fought against the idea that she must simply give her whole self over to God and let Him do it all for her. And yet, God insisted that He must do it and she must submit. She was trying to hold on to the world's ways with one hand and grasp God's ways with the other.

At that moment she realized that Fanny Crosby could not save Fanny Crosby. She must surrender herself completely to God and let Him do His work in her the way He wanted.

Light flooded her mind and heart, a light just as bright as any that might flood the eyes. The day she entered the New York Institution for the Blind was no longer the happiest day of her life. This one was, this day right here. The empty spot shriveled in the light. Jesus was the light!

Fanny Crosby reached heavenward and sang for joy.

> At the cross, at the cross
> Where I first saw the light,
> And the burden of my heart
> rolled away,
> It was there by faith
> I received my sight,
> And now I am happy
> all the day!

11

Of Elm Trees and Alexander

Spring 1857

Summer days are longer than winter days. Sometimes, though, the length of the day has nothing to do with the seasons. This had been a long, long day, regardless of the amount of sunlight. It was one of those days you wished would end around two o'clock, but never did.

With a heavy sigh Fanny closed the lecture room door and walked away down the hall. Her shoes had not been broken in properly. Her feet ached. She was wearing one of those new bone corsets which promised complete freedom of movement; it delivered nothing of the sort.

She heard giggling by the stairwell. She cleared her throat with a loud "ahem." A girl's voice gasped. Silence. Fanny passed by, smiling, without asking who it might be. The teen-aged boys and girls frequently met beneath the stairwell. As Fanny herself said more than once, blind girls need love, too.

Now and then these harmless, fledgling romances would blossom into love and marriage. Usually, they faded with the season. Usually also, they were promptly replaced by new infatuations. The web of human entanglement could be incredibly complex!

She stopped. She should first go down to the office and straighten out the new schedule for next term. Bother! Ah well. She had best get that done now; then it would be finished. First, she took off those killer shoes. Then she turned and headed down the long hall.

Music. Fanny stopped to listen. Someone was playing the piano in the music room. The melody sounded baroque or post-baroque, and yet it was no composer she'd ever heard. She paused in the music room doorway. The piano tinkled. It sang. Nimble fingers chased the final bars up the scale. The pianist shifted the same melody into a minor key. The music took on a totally new texture, something that might come drifting out from the halls of the tsar in Russia.

Intrigued, Fanny crossed the room to the piano. She listened awhile before she spoke. "And who is the artist playing this lovely music?"

The piano clunked; the pianist gasped. The music continued.

"Oh, I'm so sorry! I didn't mean to startle you. And here are my shoes in my hand instead of on my feet, where you could hear them." Fanny smiled. "But now I can reasonably guess that you are blind. Do I know you?"

A smooth, rolling male voice chuckled. "You know me."

"Oh, of course! Mr. Van Alstyne. I know you well."

"Do you remember when the institution sent a group of students and teachers out on a tour, and you stopped along the Erie Canal?"

"Fund raising, in part. And trying to get interest in similar schools. Oswego, New York, right? Ancient history, though. That must have been ten years ago."

"My mother took you aside and told you I'd be enrolling here; asked you to keep an eye on me."

Fanny laughed. "I don't think she realized exactly what she said—'keep an eye on you.' But I did mark your progress, though I don't think I ever told you."

"And your classes were always my favorites. You don't just teach the material. You explain why it is something important for a blind person to know. Made all the difference. I have always admired your teaching. You were an inspiration to me."

Fanny's breastbone tickled. She had learned (the hard way) to disregard flattery, as Dr. Jones had counseled so long ago. But when Alexander Van Alstyne praised her, it gave her goosebumps.

She leaned on the piano. "You went on to college after you graduated from here."

"Schenectady. Union College. Yes."

"You graduated from there as well, I assume."

"With a lovely degree in dead languages and hypothetical theology. Neither will make you a living, so I'm back here to teach music. I sounded sarcastic just then; I shouldn't have. This pleases me very much. Classical studies are delightful, but music is my first love."

"Obviously." Fanny leaned with her elbows and propped her chin in her hands. She listened, simply listened. He shifted to a new melody, again one she had not heard before. The music soared, rippled, danced. Fanny admired any talent, but she admired musical talent most of all, and Alex Van Alstyne was uniquely talented. She wondered what he looked like. She wondered if his face were smiling with pleasure now, or if it were frowning in concentration.

The music ended. "Are you still here, Miss Crosby, or have you long since departed on silent feet with your shoes in your hand?"

Fanny giggled. "I left some time ago. You mean you're still here?"

"Just sitting here thinking. Miss Crosby, would do me a great favor?"

"If I can."

"Dinner will be served shortly. Join me for dinner and then in the common parlor afterward. Recite some of your latest work for me. I've long been enthralled by your beautiful verse."

Was Fanny's heart throbbing? Do robins sing in spring? She stammered something on the order of yes, she would be honored. She said something about that schedule business for next term and about going to the office. She excused herself then with some hasty word or other. A moment after she stepped out into the dank and silent hall she couldn't remember a word of what she had just said.

Fanny was thirty-seven years old now. How old was young Mr. Van Alstyne? She was pretty certain he was eleven years younger than she. Twenty-five? Twenty-six? Women routinely married men older than themselves, often much older. Fanny stopped and laughed at herself out loud. Just listen to what she was thinking! Here some nice young man claimed to like her poetry and nothing more. And here she was mooning about marriage! What a dunce! How silly!

The boy was simply a young man who enjoyed classical literature enough to specialize in it. He enjoyed classical music enough to write his own music similarly. It was natural he would like Fanny's poetry. Years ago a board member named Hamilton Murray, himself a lover of fine classical poetry, had read to her many hours. More important, he assigned her classical poems and then had her write her own poem on a different subject, using the same kind of rhyme and meter. It was her classic-style poetry young Mr. Van Alstyne admired and nothing more.

She must remind herself of that and keep reminding herself.

And how she wished it were she herself the man admired!

Somehow, after that first meeting on a dreary afternoon, Fanny and Alexander Van Alstyne met frequently. Soon he was calling her Fanny, and she was calling him Van. He would play new compositions for her and often asked her advice about details. She would recite her poetry and ask his advice about details. She enjoyed this mutual artistic admiration. Van knew a great deal about poetry, and Fanny knew a little something about music. They encouraged each other. Most of all, she enjoyed simply being with Van.

She wished she could say the same for being in the school. Fanny loved this school. It was *her* school. Unfortunately this latest superintendent, Mr. Cooper, considered the institution a—well, an institution. He seemed to be going out of his way to make the place dreary. He showed no kind feelings toward the students and hardly any for the teachers. He seemed impatient with anyone who could not see, and this was not the

place for that! Fanny tried to feel charitable toward the man, but it was difficult. Her school
was a reservoir of hope and a place to lift the
spirits; it was not just a place to educate young
people. Mr. Cooper was methodically turning it
into a drab box, a place to hide hopeless unfortunates for as long as possible before releasing
them into polite (and unhandicapped) society.

Ah, but with spring changing the whole countryside, who can stay droopy? March sulked out of
the picture besotted with rain. April entered beam-
ing with sunshine. The robins sang more cheerfully. The swallows came back to the attic early
and tittered all the more nervously. No one
planted flowers in front of the school anymore,
but fragrant narcissus came up every year
untended. The violets under the trees smelled
sweeter than ever. Fanny loved violets, and birds,
and spring, and—she loved it all!

April blossomed into May, and May bowed
out in favor of June. With June came the roses
and iris. Now perhaps her spirits would settle
down to normal. Those funny little flat seeds on
the elm trees popped out, followed by tender
leaves. The grass smelled fresh.

Fanny sold several more poems to songwriter
George Root. Several of his songs, using Fanny's
words, were popular and some especially so.
Her success outside the school did not really
balance out the frustration inside. Mr. Cooper
irritated her and others especially as the term
neared its end and he demanded all manner of
reports. Yet the irritations, like the pleasures,
seemed somehow remote. Was she becoming
ill, perhaps?

June. No other month can put out a day quite

as beautiful a day as June. Fanny paused beside
a window. The sun warmed her cheek and beck-
oned her outside. Today, this sparkling June
day, Fanny must go down to the office and dic-
tate a term-end report to Mr. Cooper's aide. She
closed her door behind her and jogged double-
time down the stairs.

Fanny marched through the hall to the office—
right on past the office door—out the main
entrance. Ten strides from the door she left the
walkway and squatted down in the new spring
grass. She ran her fingers through it, then sniffed
her fingertips. Mmmmmmmm.

She checked on the iris along the side of the
building. They had nearly finished blooming. Only
the flowers at the very tops of the zigzag stems
were still open. The spent flowers at the bot-
toms of the stems hung limp and shriveled and
slimy. Fanny felt much like the iris—spent at the
bottom, yet bright and blooming at the head.

She was in the shade now. She reached up to
feel the velvety texture of the new elm leaves.
She started on, then stopped again. She sniffed.
Only one person in the whole school smelled
like this aroma; Van used a particular scented
preparation after shaving. Van was somewhere
nearby. She stood absolutely still and let her
ears search him out.

The shaft of a cane tapped lightly against
something hard beyond the elms. Fanny's face
broke into a happy smile all by itself. She listened a moment longer and zeroed in on the
sound. She reached out and down with her fingertips. Here was the low rock wall that snaked
along beside the elms. The cold, damp stones
felt almost wet. She followed the rock wall's

bumps and dips with a light touch. She'd best warn him she was coming, just in case he didn't hear her.

"Van?"

"Why, Fanny!" His voice sounded as happy as her face felt. Van's uniquely special aroma was stronger now. She could feel his presence. Without touching him she could feel his nearness; it was a strange sensation. She sat down beside him. Impulsively, she scooped his hand into hers. His hand squeezed hers.

A sparrow chipped in the bushes twenty feet away. It strung an interesting array of tweety notes together, finished with its little trill, and flew away. Almost directly over their heads, bird wings whispered in the elms. It was a robin; its exuberant song poured out in waves.

Van sighed. "So pleasant." He chuckled. "I'll bet your busy little mind is going into all sorts of poetic raptures."

She giggled. "And no doubt yours is framing marvelous melodies on a theme of spring flowers and birds. Know what I heard recently?"

"What did you hear?"

"That when you're sitting at an organ or piano playing, that your face takes on an intense expression of pure happiness. That's how they described it—intense happiness. You glow."

"They should see my face now. I can feel myself glowing."

"You're not playing music."

"There are many kinds of music, Fanny." He scooted over against her. "Have you ever considered marrying? Oh, I realize you have a thriving career with your poetry and your teaching. But is that all you want from life?"

"Oh. Well, uh—" Fanny swallowed —"well, frankly, I believe that matchmaking is pretty much the Lord's business. I've been leaving that sort of thing up to Him."

"Oh." His shoulders moved. "I suppose that's about as mature an attitude as one can find. Of course, even if you married, you would probably keep on writing poetry and lyrics. That part of your life wouldn't change."

"No, it wouldn't. I'm hopeless. I suppose when I die, I'll suddenly sit up in my coffin at the funeral and recite my own eulogy in verse. You're probably the same way about music."

"I may well play at my own funeral." Then his voice turned serious. "I enjoy teaching as much as playing. In some ways more. You know, when I find a youngster with a spark of talent—that thrills me. To develop that talent, to bring the spark to a full flame, pleases me immensely. If the youngster can't afford lessons I'll teach for free. It's the spark that's so important."

"There are many good students at the Instituion here with a spark. Perhaps blindness sharpens the ear."

"Perhaps." He cleared his throat. "Cooper knows this; I haven't told anyone else yet. I've turned in my resignation. I'm going back to teaching privately, as I did before I came here."

The sunny June day turned instantly chill. "Leave? You're leaving here?"

"End of term. Good time to break."

"But—but—"

His arms wrapped around her shoulders. "I was happiest when I was teaching privately at Albion High School. There you had to produce good results or be dismissed. Here it doesn't

matter whether you get good results or not, so
long as you keep the poor little terrors off the
streets. I vastly prefer the challenge of produc-
ing good results. And frankly, I'm tired of fight-
ing Cooper every time either a student or I need
something."

"But I—but you—but we—" Fanny bit her lip.

His arms squeezed her affectionately. "I'm only
going to Maspeth. It's just a short ride down the
pike." He laughed. "I'm not leaving for foreign
soil. I'll come around frequently to visit you."

"It's not the same." She huddled close against
him. "Out of sight, out of mind. You'll forget us
with time and we'll see you no more."

"No. Oh, no. Don't ever think I could forget
you, Fanny. In fact—" the arm squeezed tighter
"—in fact, you might even look on my visits as
courtship."

She sat bolt upright. "You mean marriage?"

"You'd keep your maiden name when writing
poems and songs; I'd insist. You're developing a
well-known name, and you don't want to have to
get the public and publishers used to a brand-
new name. But I hope you'll consider taking the
name Van Alstyne in private life."

"Is this a formal proposal, Mr. Van Alstyne?"

"I said 'consider.' This isn't something either of
us should enter into lightly or thoughtlessly."

"True." She sank against him again. Married.
Fanny had always pictured marriage as something that happened to other people. Yes, she
was ready! Right now. Yes, yes, yes.

And yet, he was right. She must wait upon the
Lord's timing and not go rushing in. Fanny was
not patient; waiting did not come easy to her.

"I've been thinking about this quite a bit," he

continued. "A disadvantage—you couldn't teach and be a mother, too. The school would be robbed of its best instructor. On the other hand, I have already proved to myself that I can support a family. That's important. But even more important"—his voice took on a low, tingling tone—"I love you."

12

Of Sunlit Meadows and Mr. Bradbury

February 1864

Fanny hadn't ridden a horse in years and years, but that didn't mean she'd forgotten about them. Whenever she could she would pause long enough to say hello to the patient cab horses, the nervous cart horses, the heavy old drays. She would rub the velvet noses and feel the sleek strength beneath their hides. Strong and formidable as cab horses might be, they always hauled Fanny safely where she had to go. She jounced along now in a cab pulled by a particularly nice old mare named Jewel. Fanny listened to the steady two-beat up ahead. The clop-clop stopped.

"Broome Street," the driver called.

The back door opened. Fanny reached her hand out and another gloved hand took it. She stepped carefully down into the icy street. "Which direction is the four hundred block, please?"

"Upstreet." The driver put his hands on her shoulders and gently turned her. "That way. What number?"

"Four twenty-five." Fanny didn't think much of cabs without springs, but she loved cab drivers!

"This side of the street, third door. Have a good day, ma'am."

"Thank you! And God bless you." Cheerfully, Fanny headed up Broome Street. Here was a small porch—and another. She tapped the third with her toe and climbed it. She groped along the wall to the right of the door. Ah! Raised numbers confirmed that she was in the right place. She stepped inside from clammy February chill into a warm outer office.

"Yes?" The young man's voice sounded crisp, cross, and businesslike.

"Fanny Crosby to see Mr. Bradbury by appointment. Reverend Stryker arranged it."

"You're early." The young man sounded as though Fanny had committed some sin. "Very well. Come along." The fellow wore cloppity hard-heeled boots. He sounded a bit like Jewel, and he was very easy to follow. The footsteps stopped. He knocked at a door. "Mr. Bradbury? Miss Crosby."

Fanny heard a muffled voice from within. The young man opened the door. As Fanny stepped into this other office she heard a third person's voice asking something behind her.

The young man muttered, "Yes, that's her. And if she's blind, I'm President Lincoln. You should see how easily she gets arou—" The door clicked shut.

Fanny smiled. The young man hardly realized what a compliment he had given her.

"Ah, Fanny Crosby. At last." The man before her sounded absolutely delighted. "I've wished for a long time to talk to you. This latest book of yours, *A Wreath of Columbia's Flowers*— superb! But it came out five or six years ago, and I haven't seen any of your poems published lately. I hope you haven't been ill."

Fanny laughed. "Ill? Sick of love, to quote Scripture. I married a music teacher in eighteen fifty-eight—March fifth, to be exact—and have been busy with wife duties since then. We have a small apartment in Brooklyn."

"Ah! Good." The gentleman rumbled contentedly. "Sick of love, eh?" he chuckled. "Solomon's Song, chapter two. 'Stay me with flagons and comfort me with apples, for I am sick of love.' Heady romance, for those Old Testament sages, eh? Reverend Stryker speaks highly of you. He's mentioned your phenomenal memory for Scripture. He told me you are interested in writing hymns. Well, I've told him a dozen times I desperately need someone who can provide me with good lyrics."

"Poor Reverend Stryker. Everyone bends his ear with their longings. I've told him a dozen times that I need some way to glorify my Lord. I've submitted this to much prayer and introspection. I'm confident I can serve our Lord well in this way—by writing hymns for you. At the least, I want to try."

"And I thank God that we've met at last. I've been reading your work, and I think you can write hymns."

The door opened and those hard-heeled boots crossed to Mr. Bradbury's desk.

Mr. Bradbury paused, silent. He grunted. "Tell him I shall see him shortly."

"Yes, sir." The boots marched back out.

Fanny stood up. "You have other appointments.

I'll not keep you longer. I'm very pleased to have met you." She extended her hand.

Mr. Bradbury clasped it in his own. His hand was thick, warm, strong. "I don't believe in shifting from foot to foot yawning, so to speak. Can you have a hymn lyric ready for me in a week?"

"I shall, with God's help." Fanny felt her face spreading into a wide grin.

Mr. Bradbury escorted her not only to the door but clear out to the street. They exchanged the usual polite pleasantries, and now Fanny stood here in the cold wind and crusty snow. Her cheeks were getting tired from smiling.

Then the smile faded and fear started to swamp her good cheer. Mr. Bradbury wrote extremely popular songs, both hymns and secular pieces. People all over America sang his songs, even now during the war.* And here was simple little blind Fanny Crosby promising the great man words for a hymn within a week! How could she have been so bold—or so foolish, as the case may be? She turned downstreet toward the cab stop.

Fanny could recognize most vehicles by their sound. She listened with one ear for the right-sized sounds. The half-frozen slush had soaked through her shoes; her feet were painfully cold. Her icy-wet skirt hem slapped against her ankles. The wind made her cheeks burn, and a freezing drizzle completed her misery. February was not her favorite month. Still, this earth was only a temporary place to live. There would surely be no bleak winters in the bright home above—no overcast days, no stinging sleet, no—

*The Civil War, then in its final year.

The smile spread out across her face again.

A cab rattled to a stop in front of her. The cabbie called out, and she gave him her address. She climbed in and bounced home. But those were only the things her body did. Her mind was elsewhere, walking through sunlit valleys and green meadows. When she stepped down from the cab she had already framed the skeleton of Mr. Bradbury's hymn. Its title would be "Our Bright Home Above."

Ten days later, Fanny found herself wading through the slop again. February was thawing out. What once was half-frozen was now totally wet, but just as cold. She had delivered the words to "Our Bright Home Above" three days after Mr. Bradbury asked for a hymn. Now, a scant week later, he had called for her again. She climbed the stairs to 425 Broome Street and stepped inside, partly dreading and partly hoping. Did he like those words enough to use them? Did he want them modified? Did he dislike them enough to end the relationship already?

"Ah, here she is!" Mr. Bradbury boomed out. "I'll get back to you in a moment, Silas. Miss Crosby, so good of you to come!"

"Oh, please call me Fanny. The rest of the world does."

"Very well then, Fanny, lest I get out of step with the world. I have a little problem here."

"Oh, dear. With 'Bright Home Above'?"

"Oh, no! My, no. That's at the publisher's already. Perfect as is. But I wrote some music— come. We've a piano right over here. I'll play it for you."

She followed his footsteps. A piano stool creaked. She laid both hands on the piano.

He ran through a few introductory chords. "It's secular, preferably a patriotic theme; something for the war effort."

"Wonderful! The people down the hall complain that I'm too patriotic. That I'm always waving a flag. I'd hate to think what—" She stopped. She frowned. She listened.

Mr. Bradbury played the piece end to end. "I was thinking of perhaps 'A Sound Among the Mulberry Trees' as a title. Something like that."

"And that's the tune."

"Mm. Let me play it through again." He did. Her doubts must have come through on her face, for he played it a third time without being asked.

She thought a few moments. "I don't mean to correct such an august person as yourself. But would 'There's a sound among the forest trees' fit the rhythm better?"

"Whatever you suggest." He spoke cheerfully, so apparently her boldness didn't offend him. Still, she must not freely correct such an important person.

She heard the outer door open. Mr. Bradbury's next business appointment had come, Silas Whoever was waiting somewhere in the background, and Fanny had heard the tune. Now the rest was up to her. She was about to excuse herself and leave when Mr. Bradbury spoke.

"What's the matter, Vet? You're just standing there with your mouth open, gaping like a carp."

Gentle footsteps crossed to Fanny. "My apologies for intruding, madam, but is your mother Mercy Crosby, a housemaid in Connecticut?"

Fanny's mouth fell open. "Why, yes. But who—?"

"You and your mother lived in Ridgefield many years ago. Hawleys'. You played tag on the green and on one occasion I tripped a bully who was teasing you. I forget his name. As I recall you were the best tag player of the lot."

Fanny wagged a finger in the air. "Wait!" She listened to his soft laugh. That laugh was the only thing about him that had not changed with the years. "Main! You're Sylvester Main! Why, that was thirty-five years ago at least that we played on the Ridgefield Green. And that dead tree in the middle—this is delightful! Just delightful!"

"When Mr. Bradbury talked about Miss Crosby the name didn't click. Not until I saw you."

"Imagine," Fanny crowed. "Two people who knew each other as children, miles and miles away from here, arrive for appointments at the same time in the same office."

"Appointments?" Vet laughed. "I work here, Fanny."

Mr. Bradbury was laughing also. "Vet's practically a partner with me. Extremely valuable. Now are you certain you have the tune?"

"With God's help I shall do my best."

Vet led her to the door with cheery words of parting. The heady glow of an old friendship rekindled kept Fanny warm all the way to the cab stop. But soon reality took over.

This was by far a more difficult problem than the last one. She must fit words exactly to complex music she only barely knew. Even the subject and theme were assigned, although she must admit patriotism was a favorite theme of hers.

All the way home Fanny felt defeated, perplexed. She was trying this time to do more than she was able. The cab stopped. She climbed down into the squishy mud and slopped her way to the front stoop. Safely on the solid steps, she paused to ...

Wait! A moment ago she was slogging through treacherous mud. Now she stood on solid rock. Of course! Jesus was the solid rock. And yet here she'd been planning to flounder through the mud of a difficult problem all by herself. For shame! Hadn't she learned by now to let go of the world and give God all? In this whole business she had not even thought to address God. She framed a prayer right here and now on the doorstep.

She asked God to forgive her for not thinking of Him right away. She praised Him simply because He, of all persons in the universe, deserved praise. And she thanked Him for giving her these opportunities with Mr. Bradbury.

She could not solve this problem alone. She could make up words. She could even on occasion compose music. But now she needed help. No, she couldn't do it herself. But with God she could do anything! She would do her best for God and depend upon Him to supply the lack.

All the same, though she surrendered herself totally to God and worked hard, it was days before she had assembled the words just the way she wanted them. Finally, she traveled to that address on Broome Street that was becoming so familiar.

When Fanny stepped inside Mr. Bradbury's office today, the young man with the hard-heeled boots sounded warmer, friendlier. "I'm sorry," he said. "Mr. Bradbury is out. I expect him back in—is that 'Sound Among the Trees'? May I see it?"

She had no idea whether he should see it. He

took the page of words from her hand. His hard heels clicked over to the piano so Fanny went, too. Sheet music rattled.

He muttered her words as he played the piece through. He was nearly as good a pianist as Mr. Bradbury. The piece ended. Did he like it or not? Silence. Fanny waited.

The young man purred, full of just plain awe. "How in the world did you ever manage to do it? I wouldn't suppose you or any other mortal could make words fit that tune."

The outer door swung open; a puff of cold air swept past Fanny's cheek.

"Take a look at this, sir," the young man said.

Mr. Bradbury's familiar footsteps crossed over and stopped beside Fanny. The paper crackled.

"Miss Cros—I mean Fanny." His warm hand pressed her shoulder. "I'm surprised beyond measure. This is amazing. Fanny, as long as I have a publishing house, you will always have work."

Mr. Bradbury was as good as his word. For the next three years Fanny wrote hymn words, and Mr. Bradbury wrote the melodies. Together they published scores of hymns. Sometimes Fanny fit words to his music, and sometimes he wrote music to fit her words. Sometimes she revised words written by other people. They worked together so well.

After the war they even took that patriotic song "There's a Sound Among the Forest Trees" and turned it into a very popular hymn by writing new words for it. Fanny might have felt proud of her work for Mr. Bradbury, but she constantly remembered what Mr. Jones had said so many

years ago. Her talents were a gift from God, and
to God belonged the glory.

By the winter of 1867, Mr. Bradbury had lost
the cheerful lilt in his voice. He coughed constantly. He grew steadily weaker until he could
hardly get across a room without wheezing.
Fanny began to wonder if he would see the new
year.

Mr. Bradbury did see the new year 1868, but
only a week of it. On January 7, William Bradbury went to his bright home. Fanny felt numb,
forsaken, as if a father or favorite uncle had
died. She attended the viewing but could not
see him. At the funeral hundreds of strangers
bumped and shouldered and pushed her. Everyone wanted to say good-bye to the popular
songwriter. Some children made a wreath of
oak leaves and laid it on his casket.

Fanny's tears ran freely. Her nose ran freely.
Her hankie soaked through. Then she heard a
voice from somewhere behind her: "Fanny, pick
up Mr. Bradbury's work where he left it. Take
your harp from the willow and dry your tears."

She turned, hoping the voice would speak
again. Who was that? She knew the passage
well, from Psalm 137: "By the rivers of Babylon
... we wept ... we hanged our harps upon the
willows...."

And now the congregation began singing.
Fanny smiled amid her tears. It's one thing to
write about God's promises; it's quite another to
remember those promises when you need them!
Grief? Yes, she would sorrow a long time over
the loss of her friend. But even as she mourned
she would enjoy the sure knowledge that separa-
tion is temporary, for this very song reminded

her of the hope. This whole church full of people, who loved Mr. Bradbury as Fanny did, was singing the very first hymn Fanny ever wrote for him. With a hearty voice, Fanny joined the singing of "Our Bright Home Above":

> They are singing with the angels
> In that land so bright and fair;
> We shall dwell with them forever;
> There will be no parting there.

13

Of Mr. Doane and Money for Chicken

January 1868

The bleakest of months is January. Thick and sullen sky curtains the sun for days on end. Grass and trees sulk, dormant, waiting for better days. The flowers don't bother to get on with life at all.

The people around Fanny did not seem to mind the clammy moods of January. Why did she feel it so? Perhaps that was the reason; she could only feel, hear, and smell; and all the touches, sounds, and aromas of January were dull and lifeless.

Fanny's good friend Phoebe Knapp claimed she knew a sure way to beat winter doldrums. She bought a bright new scarf and a hat full of colorful flowers. That wouldn't work for Fanny— all scarves and hats felt alike to her.

Bone-weary as a spent plow horse, Fanny hauled her shopping bag up the stairs to her little apartment and pushed the door open. She paused to listen. Van was gone, probably for the day. Perhaps she would make herself a pot of tea and just sit by the window awhile. First she must put away her purchases. Always there is something you must do before you can do things you want to do. Even that thought depressed her.

Van had left coals in the stove. Fanny got the fire going again and put the kettle on. She hadn't had much money for marketing today; it wouldn't take long to put the groceries away. She paused in the middle of her work. No, they didn't have a lot, but they always had enough. Enough is enough. She thanked God in a little prayer—again—for always providing enough. Whatever she really needed—there it was.

Footsteps shuffled at the door. They stopped. Fanny paused, frowning to listen. It wasn't Van; Van would come crashing in like sunlight through window glass and just as warm and bright. This person knocked timidly.

"Yes?"

A man's voice replied. "I'm seeking a woman, a poetess, named Fanny Crosby." The voice was a stranger's.

Fanny crossed and opened the door. "I am Fanny Crosby. Come in, sir."

The man stepped inside. He stopped cold and took a deep, sucking breath. He stammered. He took another breath and recovered himself. "I'm William Howard Doane, a friend of Reverend Lowry. Did you send me a poem several months ago?"

Ah! That explained all. Fanny waved toward the window. "Do come in and sit a moment. The kettle's on, and tea will be ready shortly. I am Fanny Crosby, and I remember well the poem I sent you. 'More Like Jesus I Would Be.'" Fanny went back to her groceries. She dug out the tin of tea, too.

"Well, uh—thank you—uh—" The leather upholstery of Van's easy chair crackled.

Fanny was happy Mr. Doane had chosen that comfortable chair. Perhaps it would relax him. "You seem a bit uncomfortable. I hope that passes soon, for you're most welcome, you know."

"Yes, ah—thank you." His voice firmed up. "Frankly, Miss Crosby, your blindness comes as something of a shock. Reverend Lowry neglected to mention it, and I had no idea—your poetry is so elegant, your gift so pure. And, ah, these surroundings are so humble."

She laughed. "But they're warm and comfortable."

"The plaster's cracked, the paper drips in sheets from the ceiling—"

"Oh, Van and I don't see any of that."

Mr. Doane started to speak. He stopped. He laughed. "Of course you don't. And neither should others, myself foremost. How much weight we put on mere appearances! Please forgive me for making the worst of the situation." His voice had relaxed.

Fanny knew instantly that she liked this man who took surprises so hard. "Here's the kettle shrieking. We'll have tea momentarily. So you are Mr. Doane. Reverend Lowry was so certain last November that I should send you some of my work. I had assumed, because that was two months ago, that you liked the poem—or didn't like it—and that was the end of the matter." She dropped a dollop of tea leaves in the pot and clapped the lid on.

"I was called out of town. I just got back, or I

would have sought you out sooner." Mr. Doane's voice took on an edge of awe. "I was on my knees praying for someone to provide me with words I could use. Oh, I'd received many sets of lyrics, but they just weren't right. Had I looked at your work the moment it came I could have caught your messenger boy before he left. He could have brought me to you immediately. But I was busy talking to a friend—about the dearth of good words for hymns, in fact."

Fanny poured two cups of tea. "You went to great effort to find me. Now that you're here, how can I help you?"

"By doing what you do best. Lyrics. I have no trouble with good melodies, but I need your kind of words—simple, meaningful, written to appeal to the comman man. Hope for the meek and humble. Oh—" he squirmed in his chair "—also, I want to pay you for that poem. It's at the printer's already. I'll send you some copies when it comes out."

They talked pleasantly for some minutes. Mr. Doane finished his tea. He pressed a bill into Fanny's hand as he left. From the degree of wear she guessed it was a $2 bill.

Fanny still had a bit of tea. She finished off the pot and sat down by the window. William Bradbury, who had cared so much about God and about Fanny's work, was gone. Indeed, that was probably the big reason she felt so sad; she shouldn't blame it all on January. And now here was the Lord putting Mr. Doane before her. Mr. Doane was nearly as well-known as Mr. Bradbury, and he needed the same sort of service from Fanny. The Lord had also provided Phoebe Knapp, who wrote lovely melodies. She and

Fanny had written some fine pieces together. She had heard that Mr. Bradbury's company was now to be called Biglow and Main, with Sylvester Main as a junior partner. That meant Fanny would still have a publishing house to call her own. And the company's editor, Reverend Lowry, not only used what Fanny wrote, he sent others to her.

Mr. Bradbury himself had asked Fanny to continue her work, and the Lord had said essentially the same thing (who was that voice behind her at the funeral? She never knew). Now here the Lord was setting all the wheels in motion for Fanny to write hymns—lots of hymns, hymns to urge sinners to repentance and hymns to urge God's people to greater victories. Fanny's heart filled up with thanks and praise all over again.

Fanny curled the bill up in her hand. She still felt sad. But now she recognized her sadness for what it was—simple mourning for her dear friend. The pain would ease with time. Meanwhile God was taking good care of her. She hopped up and pulled her shawl around her shoulders. Now that she had this money she'd run down to the market and buy the rest of the groceries she'd needed. She jogged downstairs and out into the street.

The January sky still sulked. Was the overcast breaking up, or was it simply that Fanny's mood was brightening? Her step was certainly sprightlier. She got to the market in no time flat.

The proprietor insisted his was the finest little market in Brooklyn. It was the market closest Fanny's apartment; that made it fine to her.

His jolly voice boomed. "Why, Fanny! Back so soon."

"A man just purchased one of my poems. Since I have two dollars here, I'd like to get the ten pounds of potatoes and ten pounds of rice. And do you still have that chicken?"

"It's not been sold yet. Shall I wrap it up for you?"

"Please do." Fanny handed the bill to the proprietor. "I believe this is a two-dollar bill, is it not?"

"Oh, my, Fanny! Is that what the fellow told you?"

"Mm. So it's only a one-dollar bill. Very well. Then I'd best forgo the chicken."

The proprietor laughed. "You can buy all the chicken in my store and then some, Fanny. That's not a two-dollar bill. That's a twenty."

14

Of Butterflies and Prison Walls

Spring 1868

Ah, violets—Fanny's favorite flowers. She
paused at a little flower vendor's stall on the
corner. "I can't think of a more delightful way to
make a living." She laughed. "All these nosegays,
and most of them are violets."

"Aye. They're in season now." The flower vendor was a lady and probably an older lady. "Here.
Let me tuck one in the button hole of your coat
here. Now you can smell it all the day."

"Why, thank you!" Fanny hurried on down to
the ferry dock. Why must New York be built in
so many different places? You had to go by
ferry regardless where you started. She was
going to Manhattan just now.

"Pass me not, gentle Savior." Mr. Doane had
given her that title two weeks ago. He asked for
a hymn using those words and that theme. Usually Fanny could come up with something useful
in a couple days. She had thought and thought
and thought, but nothing happened. Blank.

"There's Fanny! We're all here!" Mrs. Somebody (Fanny never did know her name) called out. The other members of the church group surrounded her. They all trooped onto the Manhattan Ferry. Fanny settled into a seat in the inside lounge and tried to apply herself to Mr. Doane's title. Almost imperceptibly the ferry began to move. It hardly bobbed or jiggled at all.

Fanny did her best thinking late at night, when the city was quiet and no talking or noises distracted her. Because day and night were pretty much alike to her, she didn't need a schedule ruled by the sun. Busy ferries full of happy people are no place to think quiet thoughts.

The seat and the floor beneath Fanny clunked. They had arrived. The group, chattering like a gaggle of geese, marched down the walkway and into Manhattan. The church group would be conducting services tonight at Manhattan prison. Fanny enjoyed helping with these services. She enjoyed simply going along. Jesus had said that when you visited men in prison you were visiting Him. Besides, these poor souls needed God most of all. Fanny wasn't sure just where the prison was, but everyone else knew. She need only follow along. At least she would not have to stop perfect strangers on the street and say, "Excuse me, but I'm going to jail. Will you help me?" She giggled to herself.

One moment they were walking in the pleasant air. The next moment they were crowding through heavy doors into abject gloom. The cheerful conversation hushed instantly. Chains rattled. Iron doors clanged. The prison was stone cold and clammy despite the potbelly stove in this large outer room.

A forbidding black cloud hung over the whole

group. Fanny reached to her coat collar and touched her fingers to the violet. To combat the morbid feeling of being trapped, she forced her mind to thinking of things like butterflies and spring breezes. When she was still a child, her grandmother had caught a butterfly. She made Fanny touch it ever so gently, for butterflies are very fragile. The wings were little more than fuzzy stiff paper. The butterfly did not buzz or vibrate like a fly; it flittered, and Fanny could feel the wingbeats. She remembered extending her hand and feeling the butterfly lift away, flying free.

Fanny was shown to a chair. The service began. Fanny listened to the men's voices in the emptiness before her. Many of them knew the hymn well. That meant most of them had been exposed to the Word of God; they knew right from wrong. Why were they here? Even if the prison itself were not a forbidding place, that thought would be. Butterflies. Sunlight. Freedom.

The pastor preached a lovely sermon, one Fanny liked to call "straight gospel." Some preachers tried to sneak up on the gospel so quietly they missed it. Now the pastor was giving an invitation to come forward.

From somewhere out in the congregation of prisoners, a man's voiced cried out: "Good Lord! Do not pass me by!"

Click! went something in Fanny's mind. *Do not pass me by.* That was it! Joyfully, she turned her full attention to the service at hand. How happy she was that she was taking part in this service for the unfortunates of this Manhattan prison. Most important, of course, was that Jesus wanted her to. Just as important, these sinners needed God desperately, and His Word was coming to them.

Had Fanny not followed the will of God—had she not come—she never would have heard that one sentence. An hour ago she felt bad that she could not compose anything to fit Mr. Doane's title. Now there it was, the whole poem. It was forming itself in her mind, touched by that prisoner's anguished cry. Fanny put her full mind to prayer—prayer for all the men here and prayer especially for that one inmate who so yearned for Jesus.

Two days later she sent the completed lyrics to Mr. Doane. "Pass Me Not, O Gentle Savior" became an extremely popular hymn whose popularity has never faded.

Not all the poems Fanny provided for Mr. Doane and other composers came to her with that much difficulty. Some of the best just sort of popped into existence inside her fertile mind.

On Thursday, April 30, Fanny was washing the last of the morning's dishes when Mr. Doane knocked at her door.

She smiled. "Come in!" She always enjoyed Mr. Doane.

"Fanny, I have forty minutes to catch a train for Cincinnati. I'm attending a Sunday school convention there. I've composed a tune here. Do you suppose you could put words to it? I feel terrible asking you on such short notice, but—"

"Play it for me." Fanny dried her hands on her apron.

Mr. Doane sat down at Van's piano and played the melody through twice. It was a lovely, catchy piece.

"Please make yourself comfortable. Fix yourself some tea. I'll be back." Fanny hurried to the bedroom and shut the door behind her.

As always, she knelt down in prayer first. God was the author and finisher of her faith; He must properly be the author and finisher of her poems also. She asked His help. She noted the urgency of Mr. Doane's need, though of course God already knew that. Fanny settled into the chair near her bed.

She hummed the tune through. Oops—she paused. She must also ask God to provide Mr. Doane a safe trip to Ohio. Of course, he was already safe in Jesus, spiritually, but safety of body was important also.

Safe. Safe in Jesus. Safe in the arms of Jesus. Fanny picked up a little book from her bed stand and cradled it in her hands. She could not read the words in it; she could not feel its message. But as her fingers caressed its pages her mind worked more freely. She carried a little book when she spoke, also, that her words might come more fluently. Somehow, just holding a book of words made words flow. They flowed now.

About a half hour later, Fanny got up and walked back out into the kitchen. Van's leather chair crackled softly as Mr. Doane stood up. A teacup rattled in a saucer.

"Mr. Doane, have you a pen and paper?"

"Yes. Go ahead."

"I have asked God for your safety in travel, but there's a far more important safety, and we are all partakers." Fanny sat in her rocker by the window. "It's a safety worth waiting for. Our griefs and trials are paltry compared to the glory waiting for us; I suggest this song should remind us of that—and remind those attending

your convention." She closed her eyes. Rocking
to that beat, she recited for Mr. Doane the lyrics
for his music, "Safe in the Arms of Jesus."

> Safe in the arms of Jesus,
> safe from corroding care,
> Safe from the world's temptations,
> sin cannot harm me there.
> Free from the blight of sorrow,
> free from my doubts and fears;
> Only a few more trials,
> only a few more tears!
> Safe in the arms of Jesus,
> safe on His gentle breast,
> There by His love o'er-shaded,
> sweetly my soul shall rest.

Less than three days later, Fanny's song was
being sung at the Sunday school convention in
Cincinnati. And many years later Fanny would
still claim this particular song as her favorite.

15

Of Violets and Autumn

1869 to 1875

"Without further comment I present Miss Fanny Crosby!"

My, those words sounded pompous! Fanny smiled as the minister took her hand and led her forward to the speaker's podium. She was speaking tonight before an audience of down-and-out men at a crowded downtown mission.

Fanny took such speaking assignments anytime she was asked. For one thing, she enjoyed it. For another, she could tell people about God face to face. True, her hymns brought God's message to thousands of people. But there was nothing quite like doing it personally. And because she was the famous Fanny Crosby, who wrote so many hundreds of fine hymns, people listened to her.

The room was close, the air heavy. There is a unique smell to men who have not bathed recently, and nearly everyone here qualified. Fanny didn't mind the smell, but several ladies of the church refused to come to these meetings; they claimed the smell made them ill. It didn't help matters that most of these men were hard drinkers. Now and then some drunken fellow, too penned in by others to leave the room, would perhaps vomit. They coughed and wheezed constantly.

Fanny reminded herself again how God loved these men. Jesus did not die just for "proper" folks and fancy ladies. He died for these men right here. They needed His love more than most people do because they had no other love and no hope. What a privilege it was to tell them about God and His love for them!

Fanny cleared her throat and began to speak. She had carefully worked out her remarks ahead of time. They were all lined up in her memory. She held a little book, as usual; it helped the words come smoothly. But tonight, her tongue stumbled. She forgot for a moment. She began again. What was wrong? She never had trouble speaking, especially when she was telling about God's goodness. She had best just start all over again.

"Oh, dear!" She clamped her lips together a moment. "Please forgive this lapse." She felt a sudden curious urge. Impetuously she abandoned her planned speech for a minute. "It seems there is a young man here tonight who has turned his back on the things of God and his parents' teaching. Would that young man please see me after the meeting tonight? There's something I'd like to say to him."

Now why had she felt such an urgent need to say that? And whatever would she tell that young man if indeed he appeared? No matter. She would take care of that when the time came. For now her speech was rolling along freely again. It flowed smoothly from point to point just as it usually did.

The men listening to her responded not just politely but enthusiastically. It pleased her that God's message had come across well. The service closed after more hymns and prayers. Fanny felt an excitement inside, almost a vibration.

"Miss Crosby? I believe I'm the young fellow you mentioned." The voice at her elbow was young. The edges of his words were rounded off, his speech slurred. He'd been drinking.

She held out her hand; a cool, trembling hand took it. "I have a feeling, young man, that your mother is a godly woman. You must love her."

"Oh, she is! I mean, she was."

"No, no! She very definitely is. You see, when a person accepts Jesus and makes herself God's own he—or she, of course—the whole person becomes God's. The body is bound to die, because it came from earth and shall return to earth. But the soul never dies, and it belongs to God. Here now. Let us kneel right here. I'm not certain of the words to say to you next, but the Holy Spirit knows exactly what He wants you to hear." She buckled her knees and knelt on the filthy floor. The young man had no choice but to follow; she kept a good grip on his hand.

Fanny prayed, and yet it was not just Fanny praying. She could feel God working in her and through her. She had given herself over to Him completely nineteen years ago. She wanted every move and word to be His. Still, tonight was special, as if she were a pipe carrying life-giving water from God to this young man.

The young man prayed also, and his sincerity poured through.

When they stood up his voice burst out bright and blooming, not at all like the sickly, tremulous voice she first heard. "Now I can meet my mother in heaven, for I have found her God!"

With a word and a final squeeze of the hand he was gone. What a curious thing! Fanny felt a bit confused, even numb. But she also felt a warm glow of happiness. The poor ladies who refused to come to these meetings missed so much of God's blessing!

That night Fanny sat in her rocking chair as the rest of the world got quiet. She savored the memories of the day. She didn't know the young man's name. That was all right; God knew it. What if Fanny had not responded? God would have used someone else, probably, but Fanny would have missed this delightful blessing. Or perhaps there would have been no one, and that young man would still be lost.

Fanny rocked in the quiet and put together the words to another hymn. This one was not for the lost, telling them about Jesus. It was not for the saved, telling them to hold tight and wait for the promised hope. It was for all those Christians who miss the privilege of reaching out to the lost. It was for the ladies who could be telling others about Jesus and somehow didn't do it—and the men, too!

> Rescue the perishing, care for the dying,
> Snatch them in pity from sin and the grave;
> Weep o'er the erring one, lift up the fallen,
> Tell them of Jesus the mighty to save.
>
> Rescue the perishing, duty demands it;
> Strength for thy labour the Lord will provide;

Back to the narrow way patiently win them;
Tell the poor wand'rer a Saviour has died.

Rescue the perishing, care for the dying;
Jesus is merciful, Jesus will save!

Seasons passed, and the seasons melted into years. Four years after Fanny encountered that young man, she was writing more hymns than ever. Some passed quickly, some caught on. Some that captured public fancy best—and remained popular for a long time—just sort of "came" during peaceful moments.

There was, for example, that day in 1873 when Fanny received a visit from one of her favorite friends, Phoebe Knapp.* They visited awhile. Then Phoebe sat at Van's piano.

"I wrote this tune, Fan. What does the music say to you? Do you hear any words?"

Fanny closed her eyes. She rocked the chair back and forth with the music. "I hear, 'Blessed assurance, Jesus is mine.'" Wrapped up in the lovely tune, Fanny recited off the piece very nearly as we sing it today:

Blessed assurance, Jesus is mine!
O! what a foretaste of glory divine!
Heir of salvation, purchase of God,
Born of His spirit, washed in His blood.
This is my story, this is my song,
Praising my Saviour all the day long.

In 1873 Fanny's childhood chum Sylvester Main died. His son Hugh took over; Biglow and Main

*Mrs. Knapp's husband, Joseph, founded the Metropolitan Life Insurance Company.

prospered more than ever. The loss of Vet made a hole in Fanny's life, though.

That year, too, Fanny received letters from people in England, some of them perfect strangers. They praised her hymn "Pass Me Not, O Gentle Saviour." Apparently that was the favorite hymn sung during a series of revival meetings. Fanny was now as well known in that country as she was in America—perhaps more!

The revival meetings in England were those of Dwight L. Moody and Ira Sankey. Fanny wished she could meet those two men. Mr. Moody was very famous for his dependence on God, and Ira Sankey, they claimed, had the loveliest singing voice in the world. It was ironic, in a way, that Fanny's songs had crossed the Atlantic Ocean, and that these American men were preaching there, when she, who was not about to cross an ocean, yearned to hear them here.

Two years later, her wish came true. Mr. Moody and Mr. Sankey scheduled a series of evangelistic meetings right in Brooklyn.

Normally, autum was not a popular season with Fanny. Autumn presaged winter with its miseries. Autumn drove away the bees and butterflies and summer birds. Autumn made bluejays cranky and sent the wild geese flying south high overhead; their keening complaints sounded so mournful. Autumn killed the flowers. Everyone praised October's colors; Fanny could only smell the dead leaves from summer.

This year, though, Fanny loved October. Moody and Sankey were coming. The meetings opened not in a stately church or an echoing hall but in a huge rented rink. Fanny heard the place seated six thousand people at a time. That meant that tonight, as she left the crisp autumn air for the stuffy rink, there were 5,999 people and Fanny Crosby here to hear Mr. Moody.

Would Mr. Sankey sing her "Pass Me Not, O Gentle Saviour"? She'd heard his baritone voice did wonderful things to that song. Almost instantly she thought shame upon herself. Here she was, wanting something to puff up Fanny Crosby. God knew which songs would best reach this particular congregation and touch its heart— not people in England a year ago, not people in Brooklyn last night. *The people here tonight need a special message, which may or may not be in a Fanny Crosby song.*

A voice like distant thunder intoned a prayer as the house quieted. The crowd fell silent. A reedy-voiced little organ (Fanny learned later it was a small portable pump-organ called a melodeon) provided the introduction. And then Ira Sankey was filling the whole rink with his water-smooth baritone. And he was singing a Fanny Crosby song. Oh, his voice did lovely things to it. Every word came across crystal clear, even though sound in this huge barn didn't travel well. Every note crossed the rink right on pitch.

After prayer, hymns, and testimony, Mr. Moody began to speak. It is normal that most people should form their first opinion of a person by the way that person looks. Fanny's mind formed ear-pictures, not eye-pictures. Most people comment on the way two people looked as they stood or walked together. Fanny thought of the way they sounded. Ira Sankey's marvelous voice provided a splendid counterpoint to D. L. Moody's voice. Mr. Moody spoke with a twang of a country man, a good solid farmer. He must have spent some time in Boston; his accent had that strange touch to it that Fanny heard in Bostonians. His English at times was just plain incorrect. He used country expressions like "ain't," and wrong grammar. But, oh, the power of his speech!

At the close of preaching, Mr. Moody called those who would know Christ. Hundreds of feet surged forward down the aisles. Fanny was tempted to go front as well and try to meet the man. No, she would not. People who needed Jesus Christ were crowding forward. How could she face her Saviour if she pressed in ahead and took the place needed by someone else? What if some person missed out on salvation because Fanny wanted to meet two mortal men? It was not until the next February that she finally was introduced to the men who used her hymns so often.

Did Mr. Moody and Mr. Sankey appreciate Fanny as much as she appreciated them and their ministry? She spoke often at their evangelistic meetings. Mr. Sankey bought the copyrights on the Bigelow and Main songs so that he could put them in his own hymnbooks. Ira Sankey and Fanny became close friends, too, for each admired the other's music immensely.

On one occasion late in life, Fanny recited a poem as a part of a short speech at a convention. Then she returned to her seat on the platform next to Mr. Sankey.

Mr. Sankey nudged her. "Where did you get that poem?"

"It's one I wrote for Hugh Main. I suppose it's in his vault. He must have a couple thousand of my poems in his vault."

"Hah! And I own the copyright on them all!"

Mr. Sankey found the poem and asked one of the country's best composers of hymn music, George Stebbins, to put it to music. That song, "Saved by Grace," was an instant and lasting success. Mr. Sankey was not just a fine musician and singer; he was a good, hard-headed businessman also.

Fanny and Van gave away whatever extra money they received. As far as Fanny was concerned, that was good business as well—she didn't mind a bit storing up treasure in heaven.

16

Of Horses and Very Old Ladies

1903 to 1915

Fanny stood up stiffly. She stretched a bit on her way to the speaker's platform. Somehow, today she felt like a decrepit eighty-three-year-old woman. She smiled. That was logical; she was an eighty-three-year-old woman! And winter, her most difficult season, was hard upon her. The November cold ate into her bones worse than usual.

She had a built-in topic. Twenty years ago this year, back in 1883, the Brooklyn Bridge had opened, linking Brooklyn with Manhattan. Few noticed in that same year that George Stebbins and Ira Sankey moved to New York from Chicago, the better to pursue the business of publishing hymns.

As the bridge linked two important places, so published hymns linked God's thoughts with man's sense of beauty. Fanny told some of the stories about how various popular hymns had been written; people always liked to hear them, it seemed. She told about that experience fifty-three years ago this very month, when she learned to give all over to God. She felt the little book in her fingers right now, helping the words flow smoothly.

The words had not always flowed smoothly; she finished her remarks with that story of the young man so long ago and the message she brought him at the mission. She told how "Rescue the Perishing" arose from that incident.

The audience clapped enthusiastically. The meeting broke up, and a million hands wanted to shake hers. She greeted them all and blessed them. After all, Jesus died for each soul there.

A warm, firm hand grasped hers. "Miss Crosby, I must apologize for running off after you did me such an eternal service."

"What?" Fanny frowned. She didn't remember the voice at all. And yet, there was something vaguely familiar about it. The handshake was exuberant and youthful, but the voice suggested a man in his fifties at least.

The voice laughed. "I was that boy more than thirty-five years ago. I'm the young man you talked about tonight."

"Oh, why, praise the Lord! I remember the very words you spoke: 'Now I can meet my mother in heaven, for I have met her God.' And is her God still your God?"

"Oh, yes! I love the Lord now more than ever. My greatest delight has been serving Him all these years."

A thrill of happiness filled Fanny inside. Because Fanny had put aside her planned remarks for only a few minutes, because she had risked sounding foolish in order to deliver God's message, this man had been serving God for over a third of a century!

You just never know where the seeds you scatter will take hold and root.

Fanny lived in Bridgeport, Connecticut, now. After a long illness, Van had died almost a year and a half ago. He was buried down in Maspeth. Ira Sankey's son Ira Allan was the man who now worked most closely with Fanny. So many things were changing. It was only reasonable they should. Eighty-three years is a long, long time.

Fanny rather missed her railroad boys. That was what she called the men who worked on the New York trolleys and public cars. Fanny missed the stench of crowded mission services. She missed the tickle of delight when she sat in her rocker and a good hymn came to her mind stanza by stanza. That didn't happen much anymore, though she published another book of poems, called *Bells at Evening*. That book contained some of her favorite hymns as well as poems. Most of all she missed the many friends who had passed through the gates of heaven ahead of her.

Fanny had heard that time goes faster as you grow older. Indeed it seemed that way—years ticked off like months. She lived with her younger sister Carrie until Carrie died of cancer. Then Fanny lived with a niece, Flor. Flor was a heaven-sent blessing. She wrote down Fanny's letters for her, read her mail aloud, and offered what help Fanny needed to get along. It was just like the old days in Brooklyn—whatever Fanny need-ed, that was exactly what the Lord provided.

And now, in her late years, Fanny needed Flor and Flor's husband, Henry.

In what seemed a busy and very short time, the year 1914 dissolved itself into 1915. Over in Europe, nations were warring with each other. Over here, Congress was squabbling about whether to get involved. Fanny still wore a little flag pinned to her dress, as she so often did in the past, but the flag now had forty-eight stars on it. The country Fanny loved was growing up.

February 11, 1915, Fanny didn't feel like getting out of bed at all. When you're going to be ninety-five years old in a month, you can lie in bed and no one complains. She didn't feel much like eating, so she didn't. When you reach that age, people don't nag you to eat or stop or do or don't do.

But Fanny could not simply lie there. Her whole life she had suffered from an inability to simply sit still. She had to do something with her mind, her hands, or both. She must have knitted millions of washcloths. This evening she dictated a letter. Flor wrote it down, and Fanny called on her splendid memory for an appropriate poem to end it with.

Flor fluffed her pillow, tidied up a bit, and left.

Fanny thought, for no particular reason, about that doctor who ninety-four years ago had applied a mustard poultice to her inflamed eyes. How could he have guessed he did Fanny a wonderful service? Service? Absolutely. If that doctor had not contributed to her blindness, Fanny might have just cruised through life as most sighted people do. She might never have found God, and she might never have found such a close relationship with Him. She might have been a usual wife and mother, working from day to day like her own mother. She probably would never have written those thousands of hymns. She would not have published her poetry books or the autobiographies. What did that doctor look like?

What did Fanny's own mother look like, really? Or Flor or Henry? Ira Sankey had Scots-style whiskers down the sides of his jaws, and D.L. wore a wiry beard—and Phoebe Knapp, bless her—bounding around so full of energy—what did Phoebe look like?

Fanny was just as grateful, in a way, that her sight did not return. She would meet all these people in heaven, and then she would see them completely. And now the first face her eyes would truly see would be the face of Jesus. The Bible promised. What a lovely thing to look forward to!

What did violets look like? Fanny knew they were purple, but that was only head knowledge. She had no idea how purple differed from yellow or green. She sincerely hoped there were violets in heaven. She so wanted to feast on them with her eyes as well as her nose. The clock struck midnight downstairs. It was now February 12, much too early in the year for violets to bloom. Still, she could almost smell them now.

Yes, Fanny's imagination was playing tricks on her. She definitely smelled violets. Second Corinthians, chapter 2: "We are unto God a sweet savour of Christ." Fanny was a sweet savor to God; all His saints were, just as violets were a sweet aroma to Fanny.

If there were friends and violets in heaven,

were there horses perhaps as well? Yes, definitely. Fanny thought briefly of John's revelation. John had looked into heaven. He wrote of seeing those four horsemen. And the Prince Himself rode a snow-white horse. Ah, to ride a horse again. Fanny giggled as she remembered sneaking rides on horses, back in that long ago. She didn't steal all her rides. As she was growing up she rode often with friends and acquaintances, big gang rides with lots of chatter and good times.

What did horses look like really? She remembered well the feel of them. Velvet smoothness, rippling hide, bulging fore-quarter muscles and hard withers—she imagined a horse's bare back flexing and swaying beneath her.

She had heard that when one dies, angels come leading the way to heaven. It must be a glorious way to go. More than most people, Fanny was accustomed to being led. She looked forward to it. Do you suppose, by special request, the angels might come to fetch her away on horseback?

At 3:30 A.M. on February 12, 1915, Fanny Crosby's weary body at last released her soul and let it fly home.

Yes, Mrs. Shaw of long ago. Little blind girls can indeed ride horses.

Epilogue

Fanny Crosby was honored with the largest funeral ever held in Bridgeport, Connecticut. The honorary pallbearers were Ira Sankey's son Allan, Vet's son Hugh Main, composer George Stebbins, and a family friend, S. Travena Jackson.

Children not one-tenth her age sang her hymns. And her casket was smothered in violets.